D1309280

GREAT MODERN PAINTINGS

BODO CICHY

GREAT
MODERN PAINTINGS

G. P. PUTNAM'S SONS

NEW YORK

Credits for Color Illustrations

Istituto Geografico de Agostini, Novara: Pages 63, 85, 111, 141, 169

Dr. Ernst F. Battenberg Verlag, Stuttgart-Bad Cannstatt: Page 167

Verlag Aurel Bongers, Recklinghausen: Page 59

Verlag Chr. Belser, Stuttgart: Page 177

Druckerei J. Fink, Stuttgart: Pages 53, 71, 75, 87, 95, 97, 145, 155, 165, 175, 189, 199, 213

Verlag Gerd Hatje, Stuttgart-Bad Cannstatt: Page 103

Deutsche Buchgemeinschaft, Darmstadt: Page 143

Verlag M. Dumont Schauberg, Cologne: Pages 117, 221, 235, 237

Kindler und Schiermeyer Verlag, Munich: Pages 123, 131

Kohlhammer-Verlag, Stuttgart: Page 209

Lucien Mazenod, Paris: Page 211

Prestel-Verlag, Munich: Pages 163, 179, 185, 193

Albert Skira, Geneva: Pages 101, 133, 173

Galerie Otto Stangl, Munich: Page 243

Georg Westermann Verlag, Braunschweig: Pages 57, 91, 99, 105, 137, 171

Karl Thiemig, Munich: Page 83

The Museum of Modern Art, New York: Page 161

Whitney Museum of American Art, New York: Pages 121, 127, 157, 183

First American edition 1971
Originally published in German as Moderne Malerei
copyright © 1965 by Schuler Verlagsgesellschaft, Stuttgart
This edition copyright © 1971 by Schuler Verlagsgesellschaft, Munich
Library of Congress Catalog Card Number: 70-116154

All rights reserved. This book, or parts thereof, must not be reproduced in any form without permission. Published simultaneously in Canada by Longmans of Canada Limited, Toronto
Printed in West Germany

CONTENTS

ILLUSTRATIONS

9

INDEX OF ARTISTS

12

13

Many people—perhaps the majority of us—would readily admit that the idea of having to come to grips with the painting of our century, to interpret, evaluate and judge it, arouses more dismay than pleasure. Many would expect little more from such a confrontation than from Don Quixote's encounter with the windmills. This is not surprising. For, as George Grosz said, modern painting does seem inaccessible to the average man "unless he is particularly well endowed with insight or snobbery." It is inaccessible because in its stylistic diversity it conflicts radically with what, after centuries of experience, we have come to consider the function and meaning of painting as an art. Especially it is so divergent from the traditional idea that the end of art is beauty that the question has often been posed whether painting that departs so widely from this aim can properly be called art at all.

Whether the painting of our time is art or non–art is still controversial, although for good reason the argument is dying down. This book does not concern itself with this question. It is now unanimously accepted (at least by those who, independently or guided by others, have made the effort to judge the new painting by its own rather than traditional standards) that what appears so unconventional, so radically different, so "unartistic," is indeed art just as much as all that has gone before. It is an expression of our era and reflects its specific intellectual climate.

This thesis is crucial; it points to the direction of this book. A productive confrontation with modern painting can be achieved only if we are willing to relinquish all our prejudices and give up ideas we have hitherto accepted as canonical. We shall also have to investigate the evolution and nature of this painting in search of the underlying psychological forces that find expression in it.

This book seeks to initiate such an investigation. Obviously it will be necessary at least to touch upon the artistic principles from which contemporary art derives. We do not doubt that the modern movement and its brief development up to the present day (parts of which already belong to history) represent the birth of a new style which we can call our own. We are equally certain that the revolutionary emergence of this new style right after the turn of the twentieth century in the phenomena of Fauvism and Cubism and in the first non-objective painting was by no means unconnected with what had gone before. We shall therefore have to consider late nineteenth-century painting: the works of the Impressionists and the great forerunners of modern painting: Cézanne, Gauguin, Van Gogh, and others.

But the reader should not expect to find here an exhaustive history of painting during the last hundred years or so, or an infallible key for deciphering it. A short introductory text outlines the historical development, leaving documentation aside, and discusses the essential characteristics of modern painting in its artistic and intellectual context. Brief notes are given on the lives of ninety-six outstanding painters. Nearly three hundred reproductions of their works illustrate the more personal aspects and the extraordinary vastness of their artistic vocabulary. Within the total picture this book offers then a series of arbitrarily though carefully selected close-ups—and perhaps a helping hand for anyone courageous enough to want a closer view of the elusive art of our century.

INTRODUCTION

ARTIST AND PUBLIC

Before we tackle the phenomenon of modern art, it will be useful to consider briefly an iften neglected problem which is by no means as peripheral as it looks: that is, the seemongly incurable estrangement that has grown up between the general public and the artists over the past fifty years. This calls for investigation because the stumbling blocks that prevent popular taste from accepting what art is trying to say have never been greater than today. In order to see the problem in proportion and at the same time open up an approach to contemporary art, we shall do well to bear in mind that not even a hundred years separate us from an equally revolutionary event in painting that is already part of history: namely, Impressionism. Today no one questions the historical necessity and artistic justification of Impressionism, yet in its time it was greeted with abuse and derision. Even the so-called art experts of the day—perhaps they more than anybody else—pronounced the paintings of Manet, Monet, Degas, Renoir, and the other artists as ludicrous, contemptible and less meaningful than the scribblings of children or the daubs of monkeys. Does this have a familiar ring? Hasn't exactly the same been said of contemporary painting?

The often literal parallels that crop up in art criticism of that time and our own should make us stop and think, especially when we remember that despite all the hostility and reproach, Impressionism finally established itself. Everything indicates the the precedent will be repeated, and the painting of our century will eventually win popular acceptance.

Of course this does not mean that we can trust time to take care of everything and leave the evaluation of modern art to future generations. We must come to terms with it ourselves. To do otherwise would be an admission of defeat. Experience shows that the further away we are in time from an art movement, the easier it is for us to evaluate it properly. Yet this does not give us the right—or even the excuse—to decline a confrontation with contemporary art. After all, the art now being produced is the fruit of fifty or sixty years of enormously diverse, constantly shifting experimentation, both theoretica and practical, toward an artistic mode valid for our time. We are therefore far enough away at least from the basic, trend-setting early period of modern art to examine it from a safe distance. Moreover, if we are unwilling to go along with the philistine prejudice that contemporary painters, with their untraditional aims, are all crazy, then we must be prepared to accept them as legitimate interpreters of the features of our time that determine the direction of its life and thought—and hence to accept them as interpreters of ourselves.

The painful estrangement between artist and public is now an urgent problem. Nobody can maintain that creative artists live in a separate world and do not partake of the same existence as other people. How, then, could such a cleavage ever have occurred? We can limit this question historically and turn it in quite specific directions, for it is surely no accident that the split between the two attitudes to art became perceptible in the nineteenth century. It grew more pronounced toward its end, then, as the twentieth century progressed, widened first into ugly hostility and finally into a complete breach. It is a gap few people succeed in bridging, although the recent past has shown it can be spanned.

It would be a mistake to assume that all other eras unanimously approved the work of their artists. Until the later eighteenth and early nineteenth centuries documents dealing with art (which are in any case none too plentiful) give no hint of contemporary criticism. The reason for this is that the practice of publicly submitting artists and their works to critical evaluation arose only at that time, with the emergence of scholarly art criticism ready to make historical and esthetic judgments. Just think of Rembrandt's famous "Night Watch." What is now considered a masterwork of that celebrated demigod of Dutch Baroque painting brought him in his own time nothing but disdain, for the simple reason that he had dared to follow his artistic impulses and pursue something beyond the vision of his tradition-bound patrons and contemporaries.

This case—which was probably not an isolated one—certainly does not prove that the seventeenth-century public was alienated from the art of its time. But it does point symptomatically to one of the origins of the discrepancy between art and popular taste that developed in the nineteenth and twentieth centuries: the momentous change in the artist-patron relationship.

Until the nineteenth century artists of all kinds worked almost exclusively on commission. Their patrons came from the intellectually, socially and politically dominant classes: the clergy, the secular nobility, and sometimes the bourgeoisie. They relied on the abilities of the artists they commissioned to provide the sort of work they wanted. By and large, art was the fruit of a beautiful, productive partnership. This held true even when a patron occasionally disapproved of the artist's efforts, as in Rembrandt's case. For such disagreements were confined to externals; they did not call into question the very essence and justification of contemporary art, as they later did. True, there did exist the artist's individuality, as well as personal idiosyncrasy deriving from training and temperament. Nevertheless, artist and public shared the same attitude to art. They did not have to ask themselves the confusing questions so prevalent today, such as whether a certain painting is in keeping with the spirit of the time. The artist had not yet realized that his work was part of a specific intellectual context—this valuable but nonetheless inhibiting awareness was to come later. On the contrary, the "spirit of the time" was unconsciously accepted as the only possible life style because it was the existing one. In the same way the artistic style dictated by the times was accepted as a completely natural expression.

This concord, arising out of a shared sense of life and anchored in a common spiritual center, was shattered in the eighteenth and nineteenth centuries, when the order which had survived the crises of centuries found its foundations crumbling. The background of the epochal upheaval that destroyed them lies beyond the scope of this book. Long in the making, it exploded in the French Revolution in 1789. The French people's revolutionary seizure of a freedom so precious to them but, as it transpired, so dubious and insecure, had consequences that penetrated all areas of life and thought right up to our own century. But that too is beyond the scope of this book. All that concerns us here is that the sacrifice of the old order, questionable, fragile and rotten as it had long been, largely destroyed the foundation on which art had always rested. With the collapse of the forces that had hitherto sustained and directed culture—the Church and absolute sovereignty of the king by the grace of God—the frail ties linking art to the way of life were broken. Not that creative art succumbed. But whereas it had once reflected a life lived with greater spontaneity precisely because it was not rationally understood, now it often became a careful, purposive statement of so-called cultural values, set up as goals for human existence to attain. It is dangerous to simplify, particularly in discussing an upheaval as vast as this. But one thing we can say: either voluntarily or because he had to conform to his patron's cultural values, the artist began to let his intellect determine what and how he would paint. No longer did he create in self-confident response to some unconscious and unquestioned

20

impulse. His intuitive sense of doing the right thing was shaken, partly because more scholarly analysis of the past brought home to him that a painter's style is always relative in value, just one among many equally valid forms of artistic statement.

Being slowly but surely deprived of the security of a stable world was only one of the troubles that began to beset the artist in the nineteenth century. France, then the leading nation in art, well exemplifies the other factors in a trend that affected all Europe. As history has shown, the people could not fully implement the freedom they had gained at the cost of so much bloodshed or defend it against reaction. Neither could they act as a truly culture-creating force capable of setting up new ideals to replace those they had overthrown—values that would be more than mere political slogans and that might have given art a fresh start. The absence of any such culture-sustaining force produced a vacuum which was to have dire results. Particularly for the artist-patron relationship, it provided a breeding place for all the conditions which promoted conflict between the creative artist and the public.

Simplifying as much as we dare, let us single out what seems to be the most important of these conditions. During the nineteenth century, under the impact of the industrial and technological revolution, a new class emerged: a predominantly bourgeois plutocracy. This class set the tone of social life but lacked the intellectual resources to challenge art by setting new aims. Its members modeled their taste and opinions as to what was "art," and hence deserving of support, largely on those of the self-appointed arbiter in artistic matters and molder of popular opinion: the Academy. Institutions of this type, beginning with the French *Académie de Peinture et Sculpture*, founded in 1648, were undoubtedly useful as training schools for young artists. Their aims and methods have changed greatly over the years. But in the nineteenth century they exercised an almost dictatorial control over popular taste. They set the standards by which works were judged, and to promulgate their standards they used a medium which is still an innate part of the art world to-day: the public exhibition.

In France the Academy exhibition became known as the Salon, because it was traditionally held in the *salon carré* of the Louvre. It was not open to all painters, but only to those deemed worthy of the honor by an unchallengeable jury of Academicians. In their own interests they had to uphold the principles taught at the Academy. Moreover, they were backed not only by the so-called educated class, which furnished the patrons, but also by the popular taste they themselves had molded. Those artists who were led by inner necessity and convictions to revolt against the Academy's omnipotence and to pursue creative paths found themselves in an impasse. If they were not willing to conform to the rules of the Academy, they were forced to defy public opinion and renounce all hope of recognition, as well as the material security of profitable commissions. They were obliged to follow Victor Cousin in his call (made in 1836) for art created for its own sake and not to gratify anyone's taste—*l'art pour l'art*.

Here we have the major cause of the painful estrangement between artist and public in our time. Faced with the choice of falling into disfavor or prostituting themselves for the sake of success, the twentieth-century painters genuinely dedicated to art and to their own convictions opted as decisively as had the Impressionists for their integrity. Their inner compulsions and their own free-will drove them into the isolation they needed to pursue their self-imposed aims.

THE BACKGROUND OF MODERN PAINTING

A study of modern painting must start with the question of its beginnings. And here it immediately runs into difficulty because this question cannot be answered by simply establishing a date of first appearance for painting that can be labeled "modern" in style. Although the meaning of the term varies even in scholarly usage, the modern period is generally assumed to begin with the first sure signs of the break with the tradition whose aims date back to the Renaissance. This cleavage began in the first decade of our century. Of course this is true only in a limited sense. Those ten years, the decade that was the cradle of Fauvism, Cubism, Futurism, and the earliest non-objective painting, gave birth to the first formulation in plastic terms of the concepts we now recognize as undeniably "modern." Yet this revolutionary eruption cannot be taken in any absolute sense as the beginning. Anyone with insight does not need to be told that modern painting did not emerge from the void at a certain point in time. The question of its beginnings must therefore be widened to include what we have come to regard as its foundations.

It is generally agreed that the intellectual background of twentieth-century painting extends back through the nineteenth century. But there is no such agreement about its artistic foundations. Were they laid in the last decade of the nineteenth century by the great individualists, the recognized pioneers, Cézanne, Gauguin, Seurat, Van Gogh, and Toulouse-Lautrec? Or can we trace them back to the very phenomenon these painters were revolting against: Impressionism? It is difficult to say. If we take the break with academic tradition as the turning point, then Impressionism, being closely linked to visual experience and nature, would at first sight seem totally "unmodern." And if we concentrate on its outward characteristics: the way forms in Impressionist works lose their firm contours, pictorial space becomes diffuse and vague, detail is subordinated to the whole, color and light become more important than objective reality, and movement breaks up static composition, then Impressionism identifies itself as a late stylistic development, as the finale in which a representational tradition drew to its close, much as Baroque painting did in the Rococo.

But closer examination shows that, tightly linked as Impressionism is with previous art forms, it possesses totally new "modern" characteristics which anticipate the future. Perhaps no more than accidental by-products of a particular way of painting and seeing whose full significance was not at first discernible, those features did prepare the foundation for modern art.

To discover these pioneering characteristics we must examine the aims of the Impressionist movement, which flourished in Paris between about 1860 and 1890 in the shade of established academic painting. Its very name is indicative. Louis Leroy first used it, in an intentionally derogatory tone, in a disparaging critique of the first group exhibition held by these painters in 1874. He took it from the title of a painting by Monet, "Impression—Sunrise," which he singled out for attack as an eloquent example of this totally unconventional new style. The outcasts soon proudly adopted a name originally meant as an insult. What they were trying to do was exactly what the word "Impressionism" implies: to depict the visible world as an impression received through the eye, to capture an effect in visual terms.

This is the crucial point. Since the Renaissance, when the artist seriously began to con-

William Turner · Venice

front the objective reality of the visible world, painting had attempted to depict the tangible essence of material things in all their reality. What the Impressionists wanted to render was not a knowledge of nature as experience shows it to be, but man's environment as it seems to him, that is to say, as a primarily visual experience. They were concerned, not with being itself, but with what meets the eye. And because the world as an optically perceptible phenomenon has no duration and is constantly changing, they had to find a way of capturing on canvas the impact of a specific fleeting moment which a second or two later would have vanished beyond recall. Obviously traditional methods and techniques were insufficient for this. The Impressionst's readiness to turn away from the material world as a reality composed of solid, enduring physical objects was especially momentous. Not that he turned his back on his environment and invented a new one. Quite the contrary. Wanting to capture some particular aspect of his surroundings exactly as it presents itself to the eye, before the artist's vision begins its ordering, composing process, he entered into a more intimate and whole-hearted partnership with the visible world than ever before. He became, as Courbet put it, a pupil of nature—to such an extent that he was often accused of being its slave. But the more the Impressionist painter subjugated himself to the seen world and the more he relinquished the right to organize the visible for the sake of mood or composition, the more momentous became the tasks that faced him. They led him undeviatingly in one direction: toward a radical change in his way of seeing and painting. For painting that no longer relied on the physical reality of material things and sought only to render optical effects faithfully had to come to completely new terms with the prerequisites of visual experience: light and color. Moreover, the desire to capture transient phenomena rather than enduring reality could only be realized by developing new techniques of brushwork and color—the Impressionist style.

The retrospective view can only describe what Impressionism did with these problems one by one, whereas they were actually all tackled at once by painters striving toward similar goals. What may justify our dealing with them consecutively is the fact that the artist's intellectual vision of what he wants to do necessarily precedes the manual execution, the brushwork. And for the Impressionist this meant clarifying his attitude toward light and color.

Either independently or through contact with each other, the group of artists that included Manet, Monet, Pissarro, Sisley, Renoir, and Degas made a discovery which decisively affected the Impressionist way of painting and seeing. They were led to it by first-hand visual experience rather than theoretical scientific research. This was the realization that nothing is visible to man without light, that light itself only becomes visible in the colored reflection from the objects it illuminates, and that the eye perceives light, not as a static, immutable phenomenon, but as one that is constantly changing under the influence of the atmosphere. The Impressionists now saw their task: to depict the world as an optical impression born of light, manifesting itself in color reflections, and subject to constant change under the effects of the atmosphere.

The painters were fully aware that light was their essential theme. This is borne out by Monet's description of his painting as "an experiment with the effects of light and color." To be sure, they drew on the whole visible world for subjects: a sun-drenched street alive with people, the bizarre rock face of a Gothic cathedral, a sea of city buildings, or a still life with flowers. As might be expected, among their favorite themes were objects and scenes from their environment that are, by nature, light-phenomena rather than clearly defined forms: flowing water breaking into glittering flecks of light, light-flooded foliage rippling in the wind, or the sky in its infinite variations of tone and color. Yet, solid objects such as buildings identify Impressionism even more unmistakably as light-painting. Monet did not paint the façade of Rouen Cathedral over and over again for the sake of its picturesque forms, but in order to capture the optical impression it produced in the cool morning light, in the radiant brightness of the noonday sun, or in the transfiguring half-light of close of day.

It was almost inevitable that painters who saw their environment so completely in terms of light and color should discover things which we now take for granted but which seemed sensational to both artists and public at the time. These discoveries—quite predictably—had to do chiefly with their view of color. The Impressionists challenged the sacrosanct idea that an object's inherent or local color is absolute in value and that light can merely change that color within itself, that is, reduce it from brilliant, strongly illuminated tones to darker, more shadowy ones. They did not deny that the object possesses an inherent local color, but they argued, quite rightly, that the eye never perceives this color other than modified by the particular atmospheric conditions of the moment. They then logically extended this observation from the individual object to the whole visible world. This explains why they were so interested in the atmospheric phenomenon of aerial perspective (which, of course, they did not invent): the optical illusion that, as objects recede, their colors appear to change, that things look bluer, for example, the closer they are to the horizon.

Another discovery of almost equal importance for Impressionist painting was that local color is not inseparably attached to an object but can merge with the color of an adjacent object—optically though not actually—to give a new color. Thus the reflection, say, of red on yellow can produce an orange that will be strong or weak, reddish or yellowish, depending on the quality of both the light and the original colors. Indeed an object can even lose its inherent color altogether under an influence of this kind and look green, for instance, when experience tells us it is blue.

One step more and the Impressionists began to see shade in a new way too, no longer as what might be called the negative constituent of lightness and darkness, but as an eminently colorful and changeable constituent of light.

This new attitude to color led to the realization that in a world seen as the sum of adjacent, interpenetrating color reflections there can be no such thing as black or the neutral grays so prevalent in traditional painting. The determination to capture the color experience of one specific moment had a decisive effect on the Impressionists' style and palette. Always fighting time, they had to give up the conventional slow manner of painting. To render the visible world through plastic effects was out of the question, partly because the physical object was of little concern to them and partly because the transience

Camille Corot • Landscape

of the impression they were trying to capture forced them to use a spontaneous, rapid brush technique. To do justice to the momentary visual experience, every brush stroke, every touch of color, had to be exactly right; no corrections could be made later. Also, they did not choose to get tonal effects by blending one color into another or to achieve a particular color by putting one layer of thin, transparent paint on top of another. They took their colors directly from the palette, without mixing them, and placed them on the canvas side by side or on top of one another. This explains why Impressionist painting looks so sketchy and at the same time so extraordinarily lively and full of vibrant movement.

29

Working with unmixed colors meant that the palette had to be carefully chosen. The Impressionists confined themselves to the colors found in nature: yellow, red and blue, the so-called primary or basic colors of the spectrum, and the intermediate hues of orange, violet and green. There was no place for black, a "color" which does not exist in the atmospherically transfigured world, and colorless white survived only because it occurs everywhere in nature in the form of reflected highlights.

Though this rounds out the artistic aspect of our examination of Impressionism, let us not forget that it could never have come into existence if it had not been for Courbet and Corot and a number of English landscape painters including William Turner, Richard Bonington and John Constable. The contemporary development of photography, the theoretical and scientific research of Michel Chevreul and Hermann Helmholtz into problems of light and color, and Japanese color prints also made their contribution. In Germany were painters less well known like Carl Blechen and Adolph Menzel. Although it may seem that Impressionism was an artistic mandate that stifled all individuality in its followers, this was not the case. Manet, Monet, Renoir, Sisley, Pissarro, and Degas, and their somewhat later German associates in the group that included Max Slevogt and Lovis Corinth, all maintained distinct personalities. Every one of their paintings became, in the often quoted phrase, a fragment of nature "seen through a temperament."

Our excuse for omitting so much is that we began by asking how and to what extent Impressionism made the turn toward modern painting and laid its foundations. We can disregard the undeniable fact that, revolutionary as its way of looking at visible reality may have been, Impressionism still faced the same task that has challenged painting since the Renaissance, the task of capturing the seen world, and hence stood squarely in a centuries-old tradition. We then see that its "modern," trend-setting function (which Impressionism itself did not follow up) consists in freeing color from its association with the local color of a subject so that it could become an autonomous vehicle of artistic statement. Moreover, the Impressionists' determination to put more trust in momentary appearance than in the stability of material things led them to question the hitherto unchallenged reality of the seen world. They themselves were probably unaware of this skeptical trait; nevertheless it set them on the road which the Post-Impressionists were to follow and the modern painters were to pursue to the end: the path leading to rejection of the outward world as sole, entire reality.

The work of Cézanne, Seurat, Gauguin, Van Gogh, and Toulouse-Lautrec transformed Impressionism, or, more accurately, developed tendencies already latent in it into a new view of "reality." These painters were contemporaries—their best work was done in the 1880's and 1890's—and for all their individual differences they traveled the same road. They had no desire to undo or repudiate what Impressionism had done. That they were in conflict with it is proved by their attempt to restore the artist's right, largely relinquished by the Impressionists, to intervene actively, as a thinking, acting, ordering, shaping force, in the composition of a picture. But the important fact remains that they did not try to negate the Impressionists' great achievement: liberation from one-sided concern with depicting the object before them. Indeed, they renounced any return to the purely representational and preferred instead to exploit the new freedom in dealing with the visible world in another direction. In view of Impressionism's discovery that the outward world presents itself to man as appearance, this new departure could lead only in one way: toward capturing the outward world, not as experience shows it to be, nor as it appears to be, but as it manifests itself within man himself, filtered through his alert, dissecting, organizing mind, through the perceptions and emotions aroused by his environment or the free play of his inner impulses.

Credit for recognizing this central task of modern painting belongs to the painters mentioned above, together with a few non-French artists such as James Ensor in Belgium and Edvard Munch in Norway. Whether they were guided by intellect, like Cézanne and Seurat, or by empathy and feeling, like Gauguin, Van Gogh and, to a great extent, Toulouse-Lautrec, their work set the goal for the art of the future: to make the painting a symbol, not an imitation. And since this task calls for a highly personal creative commitment on the part of the artist, these painters initiated an unprecedented individualization and humanization of painting.

Since the text accompanying the plates includes biographical and critical notes, all we need do here is outline the essential achievements of the great forerunners of modernism. First and foremost, none of them entirely turned his back on the visible world around him, as Wassily Kandinsky was to do in 1910 with non-representational painting. Yet all of them approach outward reality in a way never before seen in representational art or even in Impressionism. Man's intellectual or psychological relation to the visible is accepted as art's new time and becomes more important than the dispassionate reproduction of the outward world. This theme led the painter to a very personal reassessment of reality and of his own technical resources. First he had to make the picture an autonomous composition arising out of a mental transformation of the visible, a composition rationally organized according to certain laws of color and form. Secondly he had to heighten his technical resources into an instrument capable of "expressing" aspects of his environment as he saw it, transfigured by his own psyche.

Cézanne and Seurat were both aiming at this new type of picture, though they took different approaches. Seurat adopted as a principle an insight of the Impressionists: all appearance of color is based on the hues of the spectrum. Supported by contemporary theoretical works on the inflexible laws of color, he pursued to its logical conclusion the Impressionist idea of the world as a phenomenon realized in the human eye. He broke

32

Carl Blechen · Storm on the Galgenberg

down colors into their pure components, which he placed side by side in little dots (French *point*, hence the name Pointillism) in such a way that the colors blend, not on the palette or the canvas, but in the eye of the viewer. Thus he inevitably came to look at the physical thing in the opposite way to the Impressionists, recognizing it as something valid in its own right, something which, although entirely a color phenomenon, is subject to the laws of space and time. This was enough to make him free form as well as color from the contingency of the moment, to bring them back to their essentials and fit them, so to speak, into an eternal order. In a scene from nature, for example, this order requires the visible world to be reduced to a simplifying geometric structure. Since he subjected the

33

whole picture to this order, bringing it under rigorous intellectual discipline, he conferred on it the autonomy, the freedom from all imitative function, that is a hallmark of modern painting.

Seurat converted a small group of painters to his ideas, among them Paul Signac, Henri Edmond Cross and Maximilien Luce. He influenced Pissarro and Van Gogh and stimulated the Cubists and Futurists who followed them. But his influence was slight compared to that of a painter who was pressing vigorously forward in the same direction: Cézanne. Closer to Impressionism than Seurat, Cézanne declared that his principal aim was "to make of Impressionism something solid and durable like the art in the museums." For this nature always seemed to him the only appropriate subject. "I am still studying from nature, and I believe I am slowly making progress," he wrote to a painter friend before he died. By *making progress* he meant that he was approaching his ambitious goal of representing nature plastically—not "real" nature, encumbered with the contingent and the transitory, but true, essential nature. He meant that through the techniques of painting he was finding a valid way of reconciling the three-dimensional reality of space and the two-dimensional world of the canvas.

The momentous, trend-setting achievements of Cézanne's work now become almost self-evident. First, he depicted the physical object by means of contiguous planes of light and dark color. Through their optical interaction, especially the heightening from the cool tones of the dark parts of the painting to the warm tones of the light parts, and through their formal harmonies, these color planes resolve themselves into tangible objects, although they themselves have no substance and are basically as flat as the picture plane. Secondly—and this is even more important—the total composition is no longer governed by the scientific laws of linear perspective, which the Impressionists still observed, but by the law of a two-dimensional surface lacking in depth. What the eye per-

Adolph Menzel · Berlin Houses in Snow

ceives in receding planes Cézanne superimposes on a single plane, and he does it with such skill that we have to look twice to see how little the picture relies on traditional depth illusion and how much it remains on the surface. Indeed the viewer often perceives foreground and background as equidistant surfaces rhythmically articulated by color. Lastly, Cézanne reduces natural forms to their essential, elemental shapes, even though he always has in mind a certain specific form: a house, say, or a mountain or a tree. He once declared that everything in nature is composed of spheres, cones and cylinders—an insight which decisively influenced the Cubists, especially Picasso and Braque, who drew heavily on his experience. It is equally plain that he opened the way for modern painters by exploiting technical resources to make the picture an autonomous creation, subject to its own laws.

35

Van Gogh's and Gauguin's aim was not primarily to create a new kind of picture but to render man's psychological and emotional interpretation of nature. They wanted to depict expression rather than an impression. Although their methods were quite different and their work, for good reason, seems to be in total contrast, their ideas ran parallel. They discovered the expressive force of line, form and color, and their combined or opposing effects, and heightened this force into a vehicle for what they wanted to say. They were always talking about the sound of color, its music, magical harmony and symbolic value, and about the emotional potentialities of line. Van Gogh once said: "Color expresses something in itself. You can't get away from that." He also said that instead of faithfully reproducing what he saw before him he used color arbitrarily to make a forcible statement. Gauguin was convinced that painting is superior to all the other arts because the mysterious harmony of colors can touch the inmost soul and the painter can create color harmonies in keeping with psychological moods.

Although Gauguin did not shun the physical, it furnished him a pretext rather than a theme. At least in his mature work, he painted the fabric of his imagination or his dreams, not what he saw around him. Whatever his imagination absorbed from the outside world, like the dream material, was transformed into flat, sharply outlined, symbolically heightened shapes composed of harmonizing colors. Some of the shaping and some of the themes can be attributed to his "primitivism," his desire to depict a primeval, natural human race, unspoiled by civilization—man and world in perfect harmony. But the distinctive characteristic of his work is its sophistication: the spontaneous harmonizing of the color planes that nevertheless reveals a cultivated sensitivity. It is the reinstatement of the decorative as a positive element in painting. It was no accident that Gauguin's true heirs, Matisse and the Fauves, saw this aspect of his style as the essential one and took it as their own point of departure.

36

Van Gogh, originally Gauguin's friend but later his irreconcilable opponent, remained as closely tied to nature as Cézanne. Van Gogh, however, did not set out to organize nature constructively and incorporate it in the structure of the painting. His purpose, pursued in an agonizing, compulsive struggle to which he finally succumbed, was to lay bare being itself, the symbolic meaning of reality. Whether he was painting a person, a cornfield, a row of houses or trees, he was never aiming merely at capturing its superficial aspect but striving with the utmost intensity to penetrate to its true essence. The form which he would set down on the canvas, just as it had at last revealed itself to him, represented the basic symbolic image of that specific thing. To bring out the essence of things as he sensed it, he relied chiefly on color, not to create harmonies, as Gauguin used it, but to achieve strong, shocking effects calculated to arouse particular emotions. He did not hesitate to place complementary colors side by side if he wanted to arouse a feeling of tension or conflict. He would even change the inherent color of objects, making a tree trunk blue instead of brown, if the expression he was aiming at demanded it. His own explanation of a picture whose colors appear unnatural is illuminating: "I was trying to express mankind's terrible passions in red and green." We know that color is not the whole story in Van Gogh. He made his defining, separating, undulating, jerky line and even his brush strokes carry emotional values. But this more personal side of his art was less influential. His subjectivization and symbolic use of color made him, along with Gauguin, the forefather of the Fauves and, still more, of the German Expressionists.

Toulouse-Lautrec's contribution to the groundwork of modern art, though smaller and less enduring than that of his four great contemporaries, is undisputed. Apart from his arabesquelike line and his formal vocabulary, which established him as one of the greatest draftsmen in painting and won him many followers, his contribution consisted of making the darker side of human life, particularly in the big cities, acceptable as a theme. The point is not that his choice of subjects took him into places hitherto out of bounds to painting: into the night life and the entertainment world of a satiated bourgeois society, into shady cabarets and music halls and the shocking intimacy of the brothel. His really significant accomplishment was to use his artistic resources to make human behavior in these settings psychologically comprehensible and, without moralizing, to expose hitherto undisclosed traits in the portrait of city people: lust for life, vegetating stagnation, blasé exhibitionism, genuine or assumed gaiety. Even if Toulouse-Lautrec did no more than dissect the face of his time and milieu, his use of painting as a vehicle of psychology helped to prepare the ground on which artists pursuing similar aims would later build.

We now have sufficient insight and historical perspective to recognize that the new orientation revealed in the work of the great pioneers is not entirely a personal achievement on the part of each artist. It also reflects a common view of the world, filtered through the individual personality, which came steadily into focus as the turn of the century approached. This view was reflected in literature, music, politics, science, and philosophy, as well as in the visual arts, and the time was one of intellectual upheaval similar to the Renaissance. This upheaval is still in process. Being in the midst of it, we have no very clear idea of its course or extent. We shall therefore not attempt to define it or analyze its symptoms. The last fifty years, however, have clearly shown that this epochal process can be broadly defined as a radical transformation of man's relation to his environment or, to put it another way, as the emergence of a new relationship between man and reality that breaks with traditional concepts.

The upheaval was precipitated when established ideas concerning the structure of the world began to be questioned and man could no longer be sure that the visible world known to him through his senses is the only reality. In physics, unquestionably the most significant science in our century, Max Planck's quantum theory (1900) and Einstein's theory of relativity (1905) revolutionized ideas about the organization of the world, both in detail and in essentials. Atomic research, for instance, demolished the theory that matter, composed of tiny indestructible particles called atoms, is the basic substance of all that exists, subject to inflexible mechanical laws, and showed it to be a manifestation of energy. Psychology broadened out into depth psychology, and psychoanalysis, initiated by Freud's *Interpretation of Dreams* (1900), revealed that the visible outer world has its equally concrete counterpart in man's inner world. Through Freud's discoveries we learned that the external world accessible to us through our senses is not objective reality but a filtered, subjective reality within ourselves, and that there resides within man himself another reality existing beyond sensory experience: the unconscious.

It is no accident that the dates of these and other revolutionary scientific insights which gave man a fuller understanding of his inner and outer reality coincide fairly closely with the dates of modern painting. Nineteen hundred and five was the time of Fauvism and of the German Expressionist group *Die Brücke* in Dresden; 1907 the time of Cubism (Picasso and Braque); 1910 the time of Italian Futurism and the first non-objective painting (Kandinsky). Yet it would be wrong to call these events in art a conscious reaction to new discoveries in the natural sciences and psychology. It would also be imprecise to speak of art as having become more scientific. Many of the leading modern painters did indeed stress that the findings of the scientists confirmed what they themselves were doing. Franz Marc spoke prophetically of the art of the future as "our scientific conviction becoming form." But in the last analysis the artists, for all their closeness to science, were driven by the same inner necessity, stemming from the *Zeitgeist*, as were the scientists.

Painting was charged with a new task, intuitively recognized by the late nineteenth-century pioneers. It had to find a way of representing a reality that could no longer be identified with the reproducible appearance of the visible world but had split up into objective reality outside human perception and subjective reality residing within man. Between the two lay the broad area where these realities touch and interweave within human thought and feeling. Obviously painting could not represent this reality by the traditional methods of craftmanship. If the picture was to do more than imitate the visible, the customary ways of depicting form, color, space, and light would no longer serve. The accepted means of portraying these derived from an experience for which the seen world was the one and only reality; they were unfit for making visible any other. Hence they had to be radically reformulated; "nature" had to be taken out of them, so to speak. Above all, form and color as a means of conveying space and light had to be freed from their nature-imitating association with objects. Their inherent expressive potentialities as vehicles of the new themes of painting had to be utilized.

Secondly, the painting itself had to be defined in a new way. Freed from the necessity of imitating the visible world by representing a segment of it that in principle could be infinitely extended in all directions, it now had to present a specific visual idea. This idea, confined to the given, nonextendable surface of the painting, had to be a complete, closed world in itself. That is to say, the painting had to be conceived as an independent, self-contained entity.

Lastly, the artists were determined to construct this autonomous picture out of strictly two-dimensional media: namely, out of color freed from its association with objects, out of non-representational form, and out of line, which is two-dimensional by nature. The framework within which these media operate, the picture space, thus acquired a new significance. This picture space, eliminated in naturalistic painting by the illusion of physical space, light and atmosphere, now became in a sense synonymous with the picture.

The magnitude of this new concept and the challenge it offered to every artist to take a personal stand explain why modern painting looks so heterogeneous. Just being able to choose whether to rely on intellect rather than on emotion, whether to aim at constructional or expressionist qualities, opened up immense possibilities. Once painting was freed

41

from all ties to the seen world, its scope was infinitely broadened. Its themes could include intellectual interpretation of things, or the exposure of inner impulses, feelings and dreams, or the presentation of abstract harmonies of colors and forms.

Modern painting's first independent steps toward the new kind of picture are linked with Fauvism, Expressionism and Cubism. These movements, all very different in style and objectives derive from the discoveries of the great pioneers. French Fauvism and German Expressionism pursue the discoveries of Gauguin and Van Gogh, Cubism the discoveries of Cézanne. Without being naturalistic, each in its own way remains linked to the visible and the concrete.

The art critic Louis Vauxcelles was being facetious rather than derisive when he nick-named the group of French painters around Matisse "Fauves" or "wild beasts". It is confusing yet at the same time justifiable to retain this name instead of calling these painters Expressionists like their German contemporaries Ernst Ludwig Kirchner, Karl Schmidt-Rottluff, Emil Nolde, and others, who about 1905 were experimenting with painting as a vehicle of expression. Although the Fauves were artists of expression just as much as the Germans, they were basically concerned with a different kind of expression. At first, what they wanted to expose was not shocking or passionate emotions so much as soothing, intimate—not to say beautiful—pictorial harmony that would be decorative and symbolic rather than dramatic and provoking.

Characteristically, Fauvism's leading painter, Matisse, once compared his art to an arm-chair in which one rests from one's labors. Of course most of the Fauves, notably Georges Rouault, André Derain, Maurice Vlaminck, and Raoul Dufy, soon broke away from the armchair comfort of the program as formulated by Matisse and gave Fauvism more ag-gressive, "expressive" accents in keeping with their individual temperaments. Yet in every case their point of departure was the desire to translate the visible world.

42

Since the leading Fauve painters are dealt with in the text accompanying the plates, we need not delve into the characteristics of the movement here. We should note, however, that even though their subjects were concrete ones—a person, a tree, a table, a jug, or whatever—the Fauves never imitated natural colors and form. Each object in a Fauve painting is an artistic symbol of itself: its true significance lies in the way its contours, converted into beautiful arabesquelike patterns of line, and its color fit harmoniously into the total composition. The arrangement of lines and colored forms in relationships suggesting balance and harmony creates an impenetrably dense, tightly knit world which would lose its distinctive appearance if it were deprived of any of its parts.

Meanwhile the German Expressionists were not seeking the soothing, sonorous harmony and the air of carefree joy that characterize Fauve painting. German Expressionism owes more to Van Gogh than to Gauguin. It insistently tries to capture human feelings, the dramatic tension between man and his environment, all the exciting aspects of the enigmatic and the psychic. It has often been said, quite rightly, that German and French characteristics are clearly reflected in the marked differences between these two contemporaneous movements. The clear, rational French way of thinking was foreign to the more intuitive Germans. They tackled their problems with an often explosive passion directed by emotional insight rather than reason. The demonic and the pessimistic, psychic disquiet and uncertainty—elements that had no place in the Fauvism of Matisse—insistently thrust themselves into their work. The paintings of the artists of *Die Brücke* (The Bridge), the group formed around Kirchner in 1905, which included Schmidt-Rottluff and Erich Heckel and later Nolde, Max Pechstein and Otto Müller, may at first seem more homogeneous than those of the Fauves; in fact it is often difficult to distinguish among them. Yet ultimately the tremendous range of German Expressionism offered more scope for the individual to express his opinions and feelings than Fauvism, with its definite program and more uniform aims. Among the German Expressionists, all the similarities of color technique, composition and ultimate intention cannot obscure this fact.

It is not surprising that Cubism, the third mode of early modern painting, should have begun in France and remained, in its pure form, a French phenomenon.

By its very nature it relied more on reason than emotion and was oriented toward formal construction rather than expression. Its aim was not imitation of nature but the creation of an autonomous work of art born of the rigorous discipline of a structuring mind. Just as Fauvism and Expressionism developed the discoveries of Gauguin and Van Gogh, the founders of Cubism, Picasso and Braque, carried Cézanne's work to its logical conclusion. Like Cézanne, they stay close to the physical object, but they "take the nature of it." By perceiving it as an entity composed of multiple separate acts of seeing, they penetrate to its essence, now freed of all need for natural illumination, perspective illusion and atmospheric effects. In the first, "analytical" phase of Cubism form plays a major role. Color is often monochrome, implying light and space through its tonalities and inter-actions (not, of course, natural light and space, but the pictorial light and space). But even though the forms composing the picture are primary, they cannot be shown unambig-uously, as themselves, because the purpose is no longer to depict the subject from one particular viewpoint but to see it from all angles at once. The painter must grasp the totality of these multiple aspects. This is the essential process of analytical Cubism: taking the physical object as the point of departure and dissecting it into these multiple forms.

No work of analytical Cubism is entirely without graphic signals recalling the natural appearance of its concrete *motif*, "fanned out," so to speak, in what looks like a chaos of shapes. These signals stand as autonomous symbols, but they also help us to recognize that the picture "represents" a violin or a jug or whatever it may be. This incorporation of signs aimed at giving the viewer an idea of the picture's theme became much more important in the second, "synthetic" phase of Cubism, which began between 1910 and 1912. There was no sudden turning point, but this phase first became identifiable in the work of Juan Gris, and it took exactly the opposite direction. Its aim was to allow objects to emerge from a synthesis of colors and forms. Its intentions were plainly stated by Gris himself: "Cézanne (and also analytical Cubism) turned a bottle into a cylinder. I start with the cylinder in order to create a specific object. I turn a cylinder into a bottle. Cézanne aimed at architecture. I start with it." Here lay Cubism's true significance for subsequent painting. To achieve this aim, which brought the artist's creative resources more strongly into play, some associative clues were required. These were supplied through color, which once again moved toward full exploitation and also by incorporating physically descriptive details and stressing concrete objects in the titles of paintings, but first and foremost by the characteristic use of *détails réels*. These might be isolated letters of the alphabet, disconnected words, pasted-on scraps of paper or newspaper (*papiers collés* or *collages*) or fragments of any imaginable material. But their primary function is not to explain the picture or make its content legible. As fragments of physical reality they are supposed to prompt us to translate the painted elements too into concrete terms and to recognize real objects in them.

Cubism pushed painting to the brink of abstraction but never actually abandoned representation. Oriented toward form and directed primarily by the intellect, its creative vision ignored the realm of expression, human feelings and psychological impulses, and used color almost exclusively as an element of composition. In 1910 Robert Delaunay, realizing that the harmonies, discords, rhythmic gradations, and complementary tensions of color can arouse feelings of movement, melody, and rhythm, founded Orphism. This far-reaching movement was a synthesis of Cubist composition and the expressive use of color. Its theme is the physical world, not in its materiality, but poetically transfigured by feel-

45

ing. The picture opens itself to legend, to dreams, to pure sensation. It becomes a pattern of colors; the only thing that keeps it from total abstraction is that the color is subject to the rigorous discipline of object-derived Cubist form.

Delaunay's painting is pervaded by a mysterious dynamism of color forms. Yet movement, depicted for its own sake in works painted in 1912 by the Orphists Marcel Duchamp and Jacques Villon, seems to have become a major theme only under the impact of Italian Futurism. Futurism was founded by Umberto Boccioni, Carlo Carrà, Giacomo Balla, Luigi Russolo, and Gino Severini, who from 1910, sought for a more adequate way of conveying human sensations. The movement was shortlived—it was more or less over by 1914—and was rigorously confined within self-imposed limits. The Futurists wanted to fuse the physical world with psychological interpretations and transformations. But they also tried consciously to work into this fusion of sensory and inward experience acoustic sensations and, more particularly, motion as a sequence of inner and physical states. And so the element of time, in which Cubism had already shown an interest by combining actual forms with recollected ones, comes into play. The Futurists did not stop at the goal of linking in one simultaneous representation all those experiences of form that come one after another as one walks around a thing. They went far beyond the Cubists in their determination to capture and communicate the passage of time itself. This is why we find everywhere in their paintings signals in form and color, which, as the eye sees them simultaneously on the canvas, create the sensation of movement—be it that of a vibrating machine, a train thundering by, or other.

The Futurists did not press on to abstract painting. Their urge to remain within the bounds of human experience held them back and always prompted them to retain a glimmer of the familiar physical world, to provide fragments of material objects that would offer a clue to their themes.

46

Short-lived as pure Futurism may have been, its contribution to modern painting was a vital one. Above all, it strove to represent time by showing the successive aspects of movement. This discovery was to affect future painting insofar as it remained committed to physical reality.

In Munich in 1911 a group of like-minded though individual painters formed a group known as *Der Blaue Reiter* (The Blue Rider). Its leaders were Wassily Kandinsky and Franz Marc and it included Paul Klee, August Macke, Alexei von Jawlensky, Gabriele Münter, and, later, Lyonel Feininger. They had no fixed program; each went his separate way in a beautifully free community of interest. Out of stimulating contact with each other and with art movements in other countries, notably Orphism and Futurism, emerged work that cannot be lumped together under any "ism"; in fact, the name "Blue Rider" is no more than a convenient label. The group's intellectual leader was undoubtedly Kandinsky. After an early association with the Fauves, he systematically applied himself to completely eliminating the physical and creating a painting composed entirely of color and form, abstract yet not totally divorced from human emotion and experience. Though Kandinsky achieved this goal in 1910, the others did not follow his example but remained more committed to the object before them, which they translated into a colorfully harmonious perceptual experience in the manner of Orphism. Some of their characteristics may be regarded as typically German. Marc and Macke, for instance, use a fuller, more expressive range of color than, say, Delaunay, and expression plays a stronger role in their work. Again, Klee's use of surrealistic, other-wordly elements may be a German trait in a painter who, as he himself said, is not totally comprehensible in terms of the here and now.

Leaving aside Kandinsky, whose creation of the truly abstract picture opens a new dimension to painting, the work of the Blue Rider group proves one thing. After a surprisingly short upheaval lasting barely into the second decade of the twentieth century, modern painting had essentially stated its case and created the tools that subsequent painting, and in a sense even the Blue Rider, were to use. It is true that *Pittura Metafisica*, the metaphysical painting developed by Giorgio de Chirico in Italy between 1912 and 1915, introduced a new concept. In 1916 he was joined by Carlo Carrà. These painters detached the solid, substantial object from its logical, rational context and placed it in a "metaphysical" space lying beyond the sphere of experience. Even though Chirico and Carrà had some influence on subsequent Italian painting (and perhaps even on the German *Neue Sachlichkeit* (New Objectivity) movement of George Grosz and Otto Dix and the work of Oskar Schlemmer), they still represent only one of the two poles—the representational one—between which the main development of modern painting took place. At the opposite pole Piet Mondrian in Holland was working toward totally disembodied, non-representational painting.

World War I checked the development of modern painting but could not invalidate the insights and artistic principles it had developed. These proliferated after the war, thanks especially to Surrealism, as represented by Max Ernst, André Masson, Joan Miró, and Salvador Dali. In Surrealism, as in *Pittura Metafisica*, the logically explainable relationships of physical things lose their meaning, and dream experience in all its guises thrusts itself to the fore. In Ernst and Dali we find the natural world depicted with great faithfulness, only to be travestied, fragmented, and arbitrarily patched together again with real and imaginary material, and given a hallucinatory twist.

An exhaustive study of the development of painting since 1930's is beyond the scope of this book. Not that its development became any less dynamic. But such a study would in fact amount to a summary of the personal achievements of individual painters who followed their own paths through the vast area lying between objectivity and abstraction.

The first three decades of our century carved a path into this wide world, where every artist could follow the direction of his choice by introducing his own ideas. Particularly since World War II, abstract painting, initiated by Kandinsky among others, has unquestionably eclipsed representational art. Only in non-representational art have truly significant developments occurred. One of these at least, action painting, deserves mention as a thoroughly characteristic art form of the present time. This genuinely international movement began as early as World War II in the work of such painters as Mark Tobey, Jackson Pollock, and Wols (Wolfgang Schulze). Its fundamental aim is to free color from any commitment to form or preconceived composition. The picture is not actually painted; it "happens" in an unplanned act that is a spontaneous reaction to the challenge of paint and surface. Action painting requires the artist to start from scratch and make impromptu decisions that determine the direction the picture takes. This may sound like an easily mastered technique, tempting to charlatans because it requires no discipline. And indeed the way Pollock went about his work did nothing to disprove this idea; he danced ecstatically around a canvas laid flat on the floor and used knives, sticks or his hands to fling, drip or flick paint onto the canvas in an explosion of color. The very danger of operating so close to the brink of fraud makes action painting an exceedingly difficult art. It demands absolute honesty on the part of the painter and close emotional identification with his work. It challenges him to transform the picture-artist relationship from partnership into complete union. As Pollock once said, "the painter must be *in* his painting." This calls for a trancelike self-abandonment which looks to many people like sheer humbug bordering on insanity. Yet anyone willing to investigate the subject will find that action painting is by no means just scribbling. Whatever its technical means, it is unquestionably a very special, separate kind of Expressionism designed to submerge the viewer into the actual experience the painter "went through."

During the last twenty years the vocabulary of non-objective painting has expanded in other directions too, especially through the use of materials and techniques foreign to academic painting. The Tactilism of Théo Kerg, for instance, borrows elements from architecture and relief sculpture.

Whether non-objective painting has won out because we feel it to be the style most akin to us, we cannot say. One thing is certain: the extraordinarily diverse tendencies that have manifested themselves since the first decade of this century stem, even in their present phase, from inner necessity and are born of the *Zeitgeist*. They are thus totally justified. While we may perhaps be qualified to pass judgment on the beginnings of modern painting, which are already part of history, it will remain for future ages to decide how far it has fulfilled its task of translating into art man's radically changed relation to his world.

PLATES

Young Girl

Still Life with Fruit

AUGUSTE RENOIR · 1841—1919

Renoir was born in Limoges, where his father was a tailor. In 1845 the family moved to Paris. Young Auguste's music teacher, Charles Gounod, wanted the boy to make music his career, but his parents, thinking his future would be more secure if he learned a craft, apprenticed him to a porcelain manufacturer to learn china-painting, thus unknowingly starting him on his career as a painter. Even before enrolling at the École des Beaux-Arts in 1862, Renoir was spending a lot of time at the Louvre, drawing. By temperament even more than by training he was attracted to painters such as Watteau and Vermeer who use color in a poetic way. Yet from the start he was also open to what contemporary painting was doing; indeed, as long as he lived he was to resist restrictive ideas of any kind.

His early work, painted between 1862 and 1870, before he was thirty, shows a maturity that ranks him with the great artists of his time, Courbet, Corot and Manet. However much his style was to change, the essential Renoir was already there. "Lise" and the world-famous "Monsieur et Madame Sisley" (1868) reveal the carefree humanity and joy of living he later expressed so abundantly in his studies of fresh, buxom young women. The great change that appeared in the 1880's was no more than an outward one: bodies and forms that were formerly solid were now softened into a play of flowing color, shimmering with summer light. Corporeal being gave way to sensuous appearance, marking the transition to Impressionism, which Renoir and his friend Monet founded in the 1880's and immediately developed to full mastery. But deeply committed to the physical as he was, Renoir inevitably came into conflict with this child of his own begetting. Painting that sought only outward appearance could never satisfy him. The inevitable crisis came in 1880, bringing estrangement from his Impressionist friends.

In 1881 Renoir visited Algeria and Italy, a journey which led him to Raphael and from him to Ingres and a new firmness of concept. His new form, from which he never again departed, was large in scale, beautiful and purified of everything non-essential. In conjunction with a poetic color, it produced clear, disciplined compositions which disdained all cheap effects. All Renoir's paintings, his still lifes of fruit and flowers, his less numerous landscapes, his portraits, and his wonderful nude studies of young girls, reveal a striving for universality, always accompanied by a warm humanity. There is no indication of the progressive rheumatic disease which in 1912 began to paralyze him until in the end he could paint only with the brush strapped to his hand. He died in 1919 in Cagnes, where he had lived since 1903.

MADAME CHOCQUET
1875 · Oil on canvas · 29 ¹/₄ x 23³/₈ inches · Staatsgalerie, Stuttgart

The wife of the art collector Chocquet, a friend of Renoir's, is posed in monumental isolation, softened and enriched by the subtlety of the color, the delicate mat tones, and especially by the sensitivity of the hands and the warm facial expression.

AUGUSTE RENOIR · MADAME CHOCQUET

Peasant Girl Sitting in the Grass

Boulevard Montmartre at Night

CAMILLE PISSARRO · 1830—1903

Pissarro was born on the island of St. Thomas in the Antilles, where his father was a merchant. He attended school in Passy, just outside Paris, and later received a thorough training in business administration. Following his father's wishes, he returned to St. Thomas to enter the family business, but promptly ran away to devote himself to painting in which he had become interested in France. In 1855 his father agreed to let him return to Paris to study. His first master was the Danish seascape painter Anton Melbey, but Pissarro was strongly attracted to the work of Corot and Courbet, whose unacademic *plein air* painting led him to his own real theme: nature. He detested studio painting; from the outset he was determined to confront nature directly. He got to know the works of the English landscapists, especially Turner, during the Franco-Prussian War of 1870—71, when he lived in voluntary exile in London. Here he also became friendly with Claude Monet. It was thus quite natural for him to join the Impressionist movement, to which he remained deeply committed all his life—much more deeply than its other members, with whom he maintained close friendships.

Pissarro was opposed to any kind of restriction and open to new ideas. In the mid-1880's he decided, to the distress of his Impressionist friends, to adopt the Pointillist style of the young painters Georges Seurat and Paul Signac in the hope that their technique would help him to attain still stronger, purer effects of color. However, he soon realized that the confining discipline of Pointillism prevented him "from seeing the multiple diversity of color values," and in 1889 he turned his back on it and returned to Impressionism. In the last ten years of his life Pissarro painted some of the most beautiful Impressionist works in existence, permeated with his typical poetic vitality. Among them are views of Paris, Rouen and Le Havre—many of them painted from his window because light by then hurt his eyes. What an irony for this man who devoted his life to visual perception.

Pissarro, who liked to write and talk about the nature and aims of his painting, once said: "When I start a painting, the first thing I try to get clear is the total context. This sky, this ground and this water must be linked in a tonal relationship, and this is the greatest difficulty in painting. The main problem we have to solve is to integrate everything, even the tiniest details, into a total harmony."

THE RED ROOFS
1877 · Oil on canvas · 20⅝ x 25 inches · Louvre, Paris

Loose dotted strokes and dabs of color conjure up on the canvas an impression of a late autumn landscape. We can almost feel the raw air and the chill mistiness which rob the colors, seen in the light of the setting sun, of all assertiveness. Pissarro was not trying to reproduce natural forms exactly as they are, but rather to evoke them suggestively. Yet he captures the impression of visible things so skillfully that we have no trouble in recognizing what kind of trees these are: apple trees in front of the tightly clustering farm buildings; behind them and to the right autumn beeches, with their slim, silvery trunks. The masterful color coordination places "The Red Roofs" squarely in the tradition of French painting and in the category of great painting.

CAMILLE PISSARRO · THE RED ROOFS

Madame Camus at the Piano

Riders

EDGAR DEGAS · 1834—1917

Degas, son of a Parisian bank director, began to study law at the Sorbonne but soon transferred to the École des Beaux-Arts. As a pupil of Louis Lamothe he was trained in the rigorous discipline of Ingres, whose influence can be seen in his early acadamic paintings and in the important role that draftsmanship played in his work as a whole. He visited Italy in 1860 and when he returned to Paris he began to paint historical scenes in a classical manner. But he was chafing under the strictness of the Ingres school and impatient to break away toward a freer style and a more lively way of portraying people, especially as they went about their everyday activities. After serving as a gunner in the Franco-Prussian war, Degas visited New Orleans, his mother's birthplace. He then turned to the subjects he was to make his own: racehorses and ballet dancers. He liked to paint horses just before the start or after the finish of a race, cooling off or weighing in, rather than in full gallop. Again, in painting ballet dancers, the theme to which he devoted more and more of his time, what interested him was not the ballet itself but practice sessions, dancers waiting to make their entrance or just after leaving the stage, still out of breath from their performance. At the same time he was exploring the world of milliners and laun-

dry workers, not for its own sake, but in order to study and paint the characteristic bearing and poses of these simple women in their own surroundings.

After about 1880 Degas gradually turned to pastel, principally because he was trying to represent movement and this medium permitted him to work faster. The special effects of pastel also lent themselves admirably to what was now his overriding aim: to depict the special ambiance of ballet dancers and women at their toilet—femininity at its most beguiling. Here again, as in the racehorse paintings, he was not trying to capture actuality but the chance effect of a single moment. Degas' theme, however, was not the Impressionist one of light. Like Manet, he was almost exclusively a studio painter. He focussed his attention on the mobility of the body, which was always important to him in itself, never merely as a vehicle of color and light, as it was for the Impressionists. This also explains why he always relied on draftsmanship as well as color for depicting his momentary impressions.

After the turn of the century Degas' eyesight began to fail and by the time of World War I even sculpture was beyond him. He died in Paris on September 2, 1917.

DANCER IN HER DRESSING ROOM

c. 1899 · Pastel · 34⁵/₈ x 14⁷/₈ inches · Cincinnati Art Museum, Cincinnati, Ohio

This painting of an elfin girl, doing her hair before the glass in the cool, almost ghostly light from the lamp, is a fine example of Degas' unrivaled gift for capturing feminity. (Paradoxically, he disliked women.) The bold verticality of the format, the exaggerated

perspective, the pose of the model, the pieces of cloth carelessly thrown down on the floor do not prevent us from seeing the picture as permanent rather than a transitory impression. We accept the composition now, but it was revolutionary when created.

EDGAR DEGAS · DANCER IN HER DRESSING ROOM

Breakfast in the Studio   *On the Beach*

ÉDOUARD MANET · 1832—1883

Édouard Manet came of a wealthy Parisian family. His father, a high official in the Ministry of Justice, gave him a good education but firmly opposed his wish to become a painter. Given the choice of studying law or entering the naval academy, the seventeen-year-old boy decided on the latter. All he got out of it, since he failed his examinations, was a voyage to Rio de Janeiro, and even that was no help to his artistic career. In 1849, realizing that his son was not cut out to be a sailor, his father finally allowed him to enter the studio of Thomas Couture, a famous historical painter of the day. Manet spent almost six years with Couture, although their antithetical views produced constant friction between master and pupil. Even then Manet was constantly trying to escape from the confining atmosphere of studio routine and Salon painting. After visiting Italy, Germany and Holland, he was determined to broaden his scope and turned more and more to outdoor studies. But it was not until the 1870's, when he began to collaborate with Monet and Renoir, that his palette acquired its Impressionistic lightness and his style became freer and less heavy. Manet never lost his strong awareness of the physical, and this explains why he never wholeheartedly adopted the Impressionist style. He always stayed close to the thing before him—never, for instance, excluding black from his color register. He can be called an Impressionist only inasmuch as he succeeded in depicting the physical by means of non-representational color rather than through an academic light-dark technique or the rich use of local colors. To quote Wilhelm von Uhde: "Manet owes his greatness not to the lightness and brightness of his painting, but to the beauty of his colors and harmonious values, the moving refinement of his rich gray tones, and above all to resonant accents of the utmost sublimity, such as only the greatest artists can attain."

LADY IN A RIDING HABIT
1882 · Oil on canvas · 44¹/₂ x 33¹/₂ inches · Kunsthalle, Recklinghausen

This is one of Manet's last works. It was intended for the Salon of 1883 but remained unfinished because of the paralysis from which the artist had been suffering since 1880 and which finally forced him to give up painting. Its unfinished, sketchy quality shows how closely committed Manet remained to nature. The form is there before the painting, so to speak, and the colors are accommodated to it in the process of painting. The work reflects the acute sensibility for which Manet is noted.

ÉDOUARD MANET · LADY IN A RIDING HABIT

La Dame Sombre

Entry of the Christ into Brussels (detail)

JAMES ENSOR · 1860—1949

James Ensor, who was born in Ostend, lived to be almost ninety. Despite a meteoric start, his achievement was not sustained, and his name will go down in the annals as one of the great modern artists because of what he did in the first half of his life, before the turn of the century. After that, the extraordinary richness of invention that marks his early work seemed to dry up almost overnight, and his painting became repetitious and somewhat uninteresting. He was not very robust, and it may be that his passionate absorption in his work prematurely exhausted his creativity.

Even as a child Ensor loved to draw. At seventeen he entered the École des Beaux-Arts in Brussels where he worked feverishly for two years, but in 1879 he returned to Ostend, never to leave again. In the 1890's his desire to depict effects of light and sensuous appearance gave way to preoccupation with a threatening world of nightmare and terror. Ghostly figures, skeletons, bizarre masks, demons, and people crowding hysterically together thrust themselves into his pictures, giving them a visionary, expressive intensity, heightened always by ecstatic colors. After 1886 his nightmare visions found their outlet chiefly in drawings. Ensor's work, pathological as it may have been in origin, served as an important guidepost for the German Expressionists, who consciously pursued the direction he had taken instinctively.

SELF-PORTRAIT WITH FLOWERED HAT
1883 · Oil on canvas · 30^1/$_{16}$ x 24^3/$_{16}$ inches · Ensor Museum, Ostend

Still Impressionist in style, this picture demonstrates the sensitive, sophisticated color sense that Ensor never lost. Framed in the oval mirror, the reflection of the artist's finely chiseled face beneath a flower-bedecked hat forms a brilliant patch of light which focuses our attention on the quizzical expression in the eyes. Here there is no trace of the disquieting atmosphere of Ensor's later work. Even the remarkably unmasculine hat, with its Baroque ostrich plume, is probably there purely for its colorful effect and should not be seen as a premonition of the skulls wearing plumed hats that Ensor would later paint.

JAMES ENSOR · SELF-PORTRAIT WITH FLOWERED HAT

La Grande Jatte (study)
Metropolitan Museum of Art, New York

The Bridge at Courbevoie

GEORGES SEURAT · 1859—1891

Compared to Cézanne, Georges Seurat aroused little reaction among his fellow-painters around the turn of the century, perhaps because he died at the age of thirty-one, so that his revolutionary aims were never carried beyond their brilliant beginnings. His goal was the same as Cézanne's: to develop illusion-creating Impressionism into an art that would endure beyond the fleeting moment. What set him on this course was probably his close study of the work of Ingres, for at the age of twenty he had become a pupil of Ingres' disciple Léon Lehmann at the École des Beaux-Arts in Paris. Seurat, however, was clear-sighted enough to realize that painting's future must lie, not in a return to classicism, but in the logical continuation of Impressionism. His main objective was therefore to make the painting self-sufficient, a world in itself, born of its own color and light, and creating its space from within itself without the help of atmospheric illusion.

After a struggle lasting for several years, Seurat about 1884 discovered how to do this. Taking his cue from theoretical works such as O. N. Rood's *Theory of Colors* and Michel Chevreul's treatise "On the Law of Simultaneous Contrast of Colors and the Classification of Colored Objects," he reduced color to its basic constituents: the pure pigments of the spectrum. These he placed next to one another, letting the colors blend in the eye of the viewer instead of on the canvas. In this way he made the sense of light and space a function of color. Convinced that art is harmony, he hoped to bring the pictorial scene into the closest possible spatial relationship with the picture plane. He therefore liked to integrate his color zones into a barely perceptible yet effective geometrical framework of horizontals and verticals. And since he was aiming at permanence, he reduced objects to a formal simplicity that often appears statuesque, sometimes even lifeless.

LADY WITH A PARASOL
1884 · Oil on canvas · 9³/₄ x 6 inches · Collection E. G. Bührle, Zurich

In this picure we recognize Seurat's urge to eliminate the amospheric and create pictorial space through the arrangement and differentiation of color. The woman's figure is built up like a statue, painted in flat, two-dimensional color planes. It derives its space from the contrast between its strong verticality and the horizontal

bars of color, shadowy green with yellow highlights, that cut across the picture, growing narrower toward the top. The ocher verticals denoting trees in the upper right-hand corner create a sense of distance, limited in depth by the blue "wall" on the left. The frozen stance is characteristic of Seurat's vision.

GEORGES SEURAT · LADY WITH A PARASOL

L'Arlésienne (Madame Ginoux)
Metropolitan Museum of Art, New York
Samuel A. Lewisohn Bequest

Cornfield

VINCENT VAN GOGH · 1853—1890

Vincent van Gogh was born in Groot-Lundert in southern Holland, the first child of a pastor in modest circumstances. He was almost thirty when he became an artist, after leading a restless life going from one failure to another. Even in his boyhood his willful, unstable temperament and withdrawn character produced conflicts. In 1869 he dropped out of school to become a salesman for Goupil, the art dealer in The Hague with whom one of his uncles was associated. He was later transferred to the Brussels and London branches of this firm and finally, in 1875, to the Paris branch. But he found dealing with clients and management so depressing that he returned to London and tried—once again unsuccessfully—to become a teacher in a charity school. Embittered, he sought salvation in the Bible but his passionate attempt to become a pastor also ended in defeat. Having failed the entrance examination for the Amsterdam theological seminary, he entered the Protestant school of missionaries in Brussels and in 1878 was sent on a mission to the Walloon miners of the Borinage region of Belgium. Throwing himself into this work with fanatical zeal, he distributed all his belongings among the poor and lived as they did, until he had sunk to such depths that he was dismissed. His earliest work, drawings of the wretched people around him, dates from this time.

Van Gogh now faced the agonizing decision whether to devote himself to missionary work or to art. Encouraged by his younger brother Théo, who had made a successful career in the art business and who was to support him loyally all his life, he finally chose art. He attended the Antwerp Academy and in 1886 went to live with Théo in Paris, where he got to know most of the outstanding painters of the time and began his tragic friendship with Gauguin. In a creative frenzy he painted over two hundred pictures in two years: landscapes, still lifes and portraits. Under the influence of Impressionism he left behind the gloomy colors of his early "Dutch" period of scenes from peasant life. In 1888 he went to Arles and discovered color amid this southern landscape. But his dream of living and working there with his friend Gauguin came to a tragic end. Gauguin, an over-bearing, self-assured character, showed little sympathy for the ideas of the hypersensitive Vincent. In a drunken quarrel van Gogh hurled a glass at his friend's head and threatened him with a razor. Alone and deranged, perhaps by grief over the shattered friendship, he cut off part of his own ear and presented it to a prostitute he knew. This resulted in a stay in a mental hospital—the first of a long series necessitated by breakdowns and pathological hostility. Yet in his last two years, ending with his suicide on July 27, 1890, he created his greatest works. Painting became a means of freeing himself from his anguish and expressing what he felt. Symbolically heightened colors, passionate statement of form, a striving for expression which can be felt even in his brushstrokes—this became his language. His legacy was some of the most ardent paintings ever created.

CAFÉ—EVENING
1888 · Oil on canvas · 30³/₄ x 24¹/₂ inches · Kröller-Müller-Museum, Otterloo

Van Gogh once said that night is more alive and colorful than day, and this picture bears out his words. Without moralizing, without dramatic accent except for that of color, he has brought a street corner to life. The starry nimbuses strewn across the sky are echoed in the oval tabletops. The contrast of the bright café terrace and the darkness of street and sky and the balanced tension of downward- and upward-reaching forms are among the devices Van Gogh utilized to achieve his effect.

VINCENT VAN GOGH · CAFÉ—EVENING

Tahitian Women

Still Life with Fruit, Basket and Knife

PAUL GAUGUIN · 1848—1903

Eugène-Henri-Paul Gauguin, the son of a provincial journalist, was born in Paris, but in 1851 his family left France for political reasons. The father died on the journey, and the rest of the family spent five years with the mother's Spanish-American relatives in Lima, Peru. The Gauguins returned to France in 1856, but Paul's early taste of an exotic world may well have been the beginning of his attraction to the colorful, natural life of primitive people. The temperament he inherited from his mother reinforced the appeal, as did his six years at sea from 1865 to 1871 as an apprentice helmsman, which took him back to the South Atlantic.

Gauguin's first position had nothing to do with art: he went to work in a bank. He was successful, made money, took up painting as a hobby, and became friendly with artists such as Cézanne and Pissarro. The hobby grew to a consuming passion. By 1883 he had already exhibited several times in the Impressionist shows and was ready to break with the establishment. "From now on I am going to paint every day," he said prophetically, and indeed he was to work like a man possessed for the rest of his life, despite great material hardship and physical suffering. After 1884 he looked more and more to Brittany, with its earthy people and primitive landscape, as a source of what he was striving to show in his painting: the natural coexistence of man and world, uncorrupted by civilization. But his lack of financial success kept forcing him to return to a life of wretched poverty in Paris. In 1887 he visited Panama and Marti-

nique and in 1888 settled again in Brittany, at Pont-Aven. That same year he suffered a severe blow when his tempestuous friendship of two years with Van Gogh came to an end. Wanderlust constantly disrupted his restless life. He sold paintings for ridiculous sums in order to get to Tahiti, where he lived with the natives from 1891 to 1893 and created what are probably his greatest works. What appealed to him was not so much sheer exoticism as the natives' naturalness and ingenuous closeness to their surroundings. The rich colors of the world of tropical sunlight gave his painting the strength and form that were to prove so stimulating to the Nabis, the Fauves and especially the German Expressionists. The great unmodeled planes of pure color, the elegant, form-defining drawing that had already shown themselves in his later paintings in Brittany were now perfected. His developed style was to be one of the most influential in modern painting.

In 1893 trouble with the authorities, lack of money and illness forced Gauguin to return to France. But France could not hold him. Again he sold paintings to pay his passage back to Tahiti, where he lived and worked from 1895 until 1901, plagued by illness and despair. In 1898 he made an unsuccessful suicide attempt. In 1901, suffering from heart disease, he went to Hiva-Oa in the Marquesas Islands, where he became involved in a long, exhausting and fruitless conflict with the authorities on behalf of the natives. He died there on May 8, 1903.

MAHANA MAA
1892 · Oil on canvas · 50³/₄ x 35 inches · Private collection

This exotic island landscape, painted during Gauguin's first stay in Tahiti, shows him as an unrivaled colorist. It also reveals his deeper aim of depicting the harmonious union of man and nature. This is brought out by the two natives' unemotional oneness with their world, of which they are an inseparable part. The picture represents a sophisticated vision of a primitive environment.

PAUL GAUGUIN · MAHANA MAA

Thatched Cottages in Anvers   *The Blue Vase*

PAUL CÉZANNE · 1839—1906

Paul Cézanne, sometimes referred to as "the master of Aix," was born at Aix-en-Provence. His father, a successful banker who had begun as a hat-maker, insisted that his son receive a good education but opposed his early wish to become a painter. In 1859 he persuaded Paul to study law at the University of Aix but in 1861 finally yielded to his son's wishes, in which the boy was supported by his mother and sister. It was years before Cézanne received any recognition, although his schoolfriend Émile Zola and his painter friends Camille Pissarro, Alfred Sisley and Auguste Renoir tried to help him. The dark pictures in the style of Delacroix and Courbet that he painted up to about 1872 were regularly rejected by the Salon juries. Often close to despair, Cézanne moved back and forth between Paris and Aix. Only after the Franco-Prussian War did he gain fresh courage, largely because of the stimulating encouragement of Pissarro, who strongly influenced his work and led him to Impressionism. Cézanne, however, interpreted the Impressionists' principles in such an original way that he came close to being excluded from their exhibitions, and the public singled him out for ridicule. About 1878 he began to break away from Impressionism in an attempt to transform it into "something durable, like the art in the museums." This made things even harder for him, and he often had to look to Zola for financial as well as moral support.

Relations with his father had long been strained when the latter died in 1866, leaving Paul a considerable fortune. He could now follow his own bent regardless of material success. Throughout the 1880's and 1890's he lived in Provence, painting the Estaque landscapes, the views of Mont Sainte-Victoire, the bathers and card-players, and the still lifes—a genre he practically rediscovered—that we now recognize as masterpieces and signposts to the future. But the public, and even many artists, rejected them, failing to understand that this was a painter who wanted to re-create not reproduce, whose aim was not imitation but an autonomous picture "paralleling nature."

Cézanne constructed his pictures out of planes of a few basic colors. He made space dependent on two-dimensional forms. He broke the strict laws of linear perspective and translated the shapes of his subjects into artistic forms which still remained fairly close to nature. But his methods were neither understood nor approved. He wrote to his pupil Bernard: "One must treat nature like cylinders, spheres and cones, and bring the whole into proper perspective, so that every aspect of an object or a surface leads to one central point." It was the Cubists who, much later, recognized the true significance of these words and followed them up. Shortly before his death on October 15, 1906, his solitary efforts, seminal to twentieth-century painting, began to receive the recognition they deserved.

LE LAC D'ANNECY

1896 · Oil on canvas · 25 x 31¹/₂ inches · Courtauld Institute of Art, London

In 1896 Cézanne lived for a short time in Talloires on the Lac d'Annecy, where he painted some of his most beautiful and mature landscapes. His transparent color planes, limited to blue, green and ocher, do not try to reproduce natural space but resolve themselves into pictorial space. The objects are flat and two-dimensional, not shown in depth. He works in partnership with nature, creating not a mere imitation but a rationally thought-out counterpart to the visible reality.

68

PAUL CÉZANNE · LE LAC D'ANNECY

Mallarmé's House in Valvins

Reading

ÉDOUARD VUILLARD · 1868—1940

Édouard Vuillard, the son of a tax collector, was born in Cuiseaux, Saône-et-Loire, and taken to Paris by his widowed mother as a young child. At the Lycée Condorcet he got to know Ker-Xavier Roussel, who persuaded him to become a painter, and they attended the Académie Julian and later the École des Beaux-Arts together. After meeting Pierre Bonnard, Vuillard began to paint in a style influenced by Gauguin's, being affected more by Gauguin's color than his flat, two-dimensional technique. Around 1890 he adopted many of the aims and ideas of the Nabis and was already exploring the themes he would later concentrate on: events in day-to-day family life in a peaceful bourgeois milieu. He stayed within this limited range for the rest of his life.

Vuillard kept to subdued colors, but the original denseness of his painting soon gave way to an Impressionistic looseness, which evoked from even the simplest subjects a harmonious magic. This persisted even when he adopted a rougher, heavier brush technique and more pronounced color contrast. Although his figures often look like ethereal beings trying to merge with their radiant surroundings, they are still very much of this world and, like Vuillard's work as a whole, present a decorative aspect of life.

HENRI DE TOULOUSE-LAUTREC
1896 · Oil on canvas · 15¹/₂ x 11³/₄ inches · Museum of Art, Albi

This quick sketch of the crippled, dwarflike figure of Vuillard's colleague is an early work. The big planes of pure color, almost unrelieved by drawing or modeling, suggest Gauguin. Obviously Vuillard was more concerned with decorative accent and color harmony than with the individuality of his model. Nevertheless, he has captured a real feeling of identity.

ÉDOUARD VUILLARD · HENRI DE TOULOUSE-LAUTREC

Dancers at the Moulin Rouge

Monsieur Louis Pascal

HENRI DE TOULOUSE-LAUTREC · 1864—1901

Henri de Toulouse-Lautrec, scion of one of the oldest and most respected families in the French aristocracy, was born in 1864 in Albi in the South of France. Even as a child he showed a talent for drawing. This delicate, weakly boy might never have become a painter however if it had not been for two accidents in the year 1878 in which both his legs were broken. While his torso developed normally, his legs failed to grow, and his figure became grotesque. His full height was only four feet six inches, and his crippled legs could not support his heavy body without the aid of a cane. This handicap kept him isolated within his family yet made him unfit for their way of life, so he was thrown back upon his natural talent and became a painter. During his last year at school he filled sketchbook after sketchbook with drawings of all conceivable subjects.

In 1882 he began to study painting in Paris, first with Bonnat, then with Cormon. Academic training improved his technical skill but was less important in his development than his encounter with Parisian artists and their work, particularly Degas. From him he learned to recognize the unusual, characteristic aspects of modern life and discovered the artistic potentialities of contemporary subjects such as the world of the *bal musette* and the café, of dancers and laundry workers. It is not surprising that Lautrec should have found his themes in the milieu he was prepared to live in: the world of the Moulin Rouge and the Moulin de la Galette, of cafés and cabarets, of actors and performers, and of brothels. Many close friendships linked him to this world and its inhabitants, and he painted it in the style he had finally arrived at around 1888, after putting Impressionism behind him. The essentials of his style are large areas of color within a framework of expressive, arabesquelike outlines, and a brush technique which suggests the corporality and superficial structure of objects through strokes of paint applied in a dense network.

Lautrec's aim was never faithful imitation. He was obsessed with capturing the life or character of his model directly, in all its essentials, not merely as it appears to the eye. He stylized draftsmanship and color to gain telling and realistic documentary effects. But his mania for direct contact with life finally overtaxed his delicate constitution. His habits became more and more dissolute; he spent his nights in the cabarets and dancehalls of Montmartre and began to drink too much. By 1897 he was obviously in precarious health, and in 1899 he suffered a complete breakdown, from which, however, he quickly recovered. But his work had lost its fascinating rhythm. It became more "painterly" and showed an uncertainty it had never had before. In March, 1901, came another breakdown, and this time Lautrec did not recover. He died on September 9, 1901, at the age of thirty-seven.

THE MILLINER
1900 · Oil on canvas · 23³/₄ x 19¹/₈ inches · Museum of Art, Albi

This remarkably psychological portrait, painted in Paris as a tribute to Renée Vert, an old friend of Lautrec's who kept a hat shop in Montmartre, marks the transition to Lautrec's final period. Blocked out in large color areas of blue and yellow, the painting already begins to show a decline in vitality of draftsmanship as compared to earlier works.

HENRI DE TOULOUSE-LAUTREC · THE MILLINER

Young People on the Beach

Woodcutter

EDVARD MUNCH · 1863—1944

Edvard Munch was born in Loyten in southern Norway. Through travel and scholarships he acquired a well-rounded art training and a good knowledge of late nineteenth-century French, German and Italian painting. From 1887 to 1892 he lived in Paris, where he became familiar with the work of Gauguin, Van Gogh and Seurat. But although he fell under their spell from time to time, by the 1880's Munch was already painting in the completely individual style that was to mark his work for the next thirty years—a style from which the German Expressionists derived great stimulus. Its general purpose was to give all aspects of appearance represented in the picture a symbolic, emotional quality. His theme can be summed up as fear of life and death, of being imprisoned in an oppressive, frightening world in which serenity, light and human freedom have no place. Violet and dark blue, the colors of life-denying night, dominate his palette. Physical objects are reduced more and more to symbolic forms.

Munch's first official exhibition, held in Berlin in 1892, precipitated such a scandal that it had to close the day after it opened. It was all too new, this art of expression and psychological intuition, which the group of artists in Dresden known as *Die Brücke* (The Bridge) and the Expressionists would soon recognize as a justification and stimulus for what they were trying to do.

In 1908 Munch suffered a physical collapse; after a long illness he became able to confront life in a new, more positive spirit. This is reflected in a stylistic change. His colors became lighter; his palette included light blue, red, and a bright green; psychological problems gave way to a more universal humanity. A monumental element also appeared and persisted to the end.

NORTH SEA BEACH NEAR OSLO
1901 · Oil on canvas · 27¹/₄ x 39 inches · Kunsthalle, Mannheim

This picture, painted chiefly in blues and violets, arouses a frightening feeling of oppression. We are not tempted to explore this North Sea beach. On the contrary we are drawn into the isolation of the tiny human figure exposed to the mercy of a threatening, all-powerful nature. The rounded forms of trees and bushes dog his aimless footsteps like ghosts. An oval fjord island hangs menacingly over him, looking more like a gigantic animal from some other world than any natural object. Man is hopelessly trapped.

EDVARD MUNCH · NORTH SEA BEACH NEAR OSLO

Old People's Home in Amsterdam   *Eva*

MAX LIEBERMANN · 1847—1935

Until the 1880's Max Liebermann, who was born in Berlin, followed the beaten track of academic genre painting and realism. From 1867 to 1868 he attended the Berlin Academy and studied with Karl Steffeck, the painter of horses; then he attended the Weimar School of Art until 1872. From 1873 to 1878 he lived in Paris. Liebermann was influenced, at least in his choice of themes, by the socially oriented painting of Millet, and for a long time one of his chief subjects was poor people. Artistically he was more strongly drawn to late Baroque Dutch painting, especially Frans Hals, whom he often copied.

During these years of travel and study Liebermann had no consistent style of his own. When he moved to Berlin in 1884 after living in Munich for six years and getting to know the work of Wilhelm Leibl, his painting and graphic work began to develop a more individual accent. He turned to milieu studies with a socially critical slant. Using full colors more and more sparingly, he worked chiefly in hazy tones dominated by gray, developing a personal, appealing style, heightened by a more impulsive impasto brush technique.

Not until 1890 did Liebermann confront Impressionism, and then he applied himself to its color problems rather than its themes. His palette grew richer, his paintings lighter and more serene—although they never became sheer outbursts of color unrelated to physical reality like the works of the French Impressionists or acquired the expressiveness of a painter like Lovis Corinth.

THE PARROT MAN
1902 · Oil on canvas · 42³/₄ x 28 inches · Folkwang Museum, Essen

A simple workman in the uniform of the Amsterdam Zoo, showing off his brightly colored parrots to an invisible audience (the painter), recalls Liebermann's fondness for popular themes. But Liebermann is much more interested in color and light than in subject matter.

Attention focuses on the brilliant patches of sunlight on path and grass, the rich colors of the parrots' plumage, intensified by the fluttering of their wings, and the gleaming white garments and hats in the background.

MAX LIEBERMANN · THE PARROT MAN

Vineyard in Spring

Still Life with Fruit

ANDRÉ DERAIN · 1880—1954

André Derain was born in Chatou, Seine-et-Oise. His father, a baker, wanted him to become an engineer, but even as a boy he showed a strong interest in painting. At the turn of the century Derain got to know Matisse and Vlaminck in Paris, encountered Fauvism and eagerly responded to its enthusiasm for pure color. His own work, chiefly landscapes, was Fauve in spirit until about 1908, when he changed direction under the influence of Cézanne and as a result of his own experiments with woodcuts and sculpture. Derain was close the Cubism without being captivated by it; it probably strengthened his determination to continue along Cézanne's road. He never strayed far from visible reality, but like Cézanne wanted to give it solidity and make it an organic part of the picture-space in a structure built up of two-dimensional elements that would be independent of natural atmosphere and perspective. In his landscapes, still lifes and portraits natural objects retain their full individuality but acquire uniqueness, an effect he gains partly by reducing the color to shades of dark brown, blue and green.

Derain also made woodcuts and drawings for book illustrations and was an excellent theater and ballet designer. He died in Garches in 1954 as the result of an automobile accident.

COLLIOURE—VILLAGE AND SEA
1904—1905 · Oil on canvas · 25³/₈ x 31¹/₂ inches · Folkwang Museum, Essen

This charming landscape from Derain's Fauve period gets its effect from the juxtaposition of full-toned colors, chiefly red, ocher and blue. Touches of black and white skillfully introduced in the cluster of houses provide lively accents, while the three trees add depth to a painting which lacks natural atmosphere. The various areas are full of detail and are outlined and held together by long, irregular lines that organize the painting and give it a harmony and tranquillity that transcend the strong notes of color.

ANDRÉ DERAIN · COLLIOURE—VILLAGE AND SEA

Madame Matisse (The Green Line)

The Manila Shawl

HENRI MATISSE · 1869—1954

Matisse's parents wanted him to study law, but in 1890 he took up painting. He received his elementary training in Paris at the Académie Julian (1892) and the École des Beaux-Arts (1893). His early works, first exhibited in 1896, featured the discreet colors he had used in copying the old masters. Impressionism did not affect him much, except for lightening his palette. Toward the turn of the century the works of Renoir and Cézanne, his collaboration with his lifetime friend Albert Marquet, and his contact with Paul Bonnard, André Derain and Maurice Vlaminck all led him toward color, which became the essential element in his painting. About 1904 he made some brief essays in Pointillism, but he had no affinity for its methods and soon relinquished it in favor of a style that relied on large unmodeled areas of pure color. Landscapes of Collioure and Saint-Tropez illustrate this phase.

In 1905 came the real turning point. The autumn Salon of that year, which included paintings by Matisse, Derain, Vlaminck, Henri Manguin, and Georges Rouault, announced the birth of the school which Matisse was to head: the Fauves. His picture entitled "Luxe, Calme et Volupté" formulated this new movement's program: to construct paintings out of big planes of pure color, framed and rhythmically interconnected by arabesquelike lines and brought into harmonious balance by means of rigorous composition and color coordination. Matisse's one aim was to achieve a beautiful effect—decorative art in the best sense. Anything like expresion was irrelevant to him. He said in 1908: "What I dream of is balance, purity and serenity, free from troubling or distracting subject matter—something like a comfortable armchair in which one can rest." He pursued this dream in landscapes, in his many paintings of young girls, and in still lifes. The initial exaggerations were soon toned down, as with all the other Fauves, and from time to time he drew closer to reality, but never at the expense of harmonious color.

About 1936 Matisse, widely known and admired, began to return to his Fauve beginnings, drawing on his years of experience to create works that are among the greatest he—or any of the Fauves—ever painted. He died at eighty-five in Cimiez near Nice.

STREET IN ALGIERS
1906 · Oil on canvas · 13¼ x 16 inches · Statens Museum for Kunst, Copenhagen

Matisse's quick brush has effortlessly captured this street, brilliantly illuminated by the clear African sunshine. Everything has the transparency of a water color. The painting is reminiscent of Impressionism in that the scene has obviously been sketched from nature. The arabesquelike outlining so important to pure Fauvism, and especially to Matisse, is missing. Nevertheless the condensation of the representational elements into great unmodeled areas of one color and the delicate tonal harmonies illustrate Fauvism's sophistication and structural methods. This painting hints at Matisse's joy in light and color.

HENRI MATISSE · STREET IN ALGIERS

Boulevard de la Madeleine   The Easel, Algiers

ALBERT MARQUET · 1875—1947

Albert Marquet, a native of Bordeaux, went to live in Paris in 1890 and studied at the École des Arts Decoratifs; in 1897 he entered the École des Beaux-Arts. He was closely associated with the Fauves and was the lifelong friend of their leader, Henri Matisse, but he soon turned his back on pure Fauvism in favor of a more naturalistic style, sobering down the forceful, symbolic colors. He has a passionate love of travel; besides his native France he knew North Africa, Italy, Norway, and Germany. The theme of his personal brand of Fauvism was his own richly varied impressions of landscape, especially of towns and harbors. The appealing charm of his pictures soon brought him admirers and an income sufficient to indulge his love of travel, which toward the end of his life took him to Algeria and the Soviet Union. His readily accessible compositions continue to hold their audience.

THE BEACH AT FÉCAMP
1906 · Oil on canvas · 19⁷/₈ x 23³/₄ inches · Musée National d'Art Moderne, Paris

Above all else Marquet loved the sea and its coasts and harbors; almost invariably his subjects have some connection with water. This plate shows a view of the Channel coast near Fécamp, not far from Le Havre. In drastically simplified forms and color which looks airy and light although the paint is densely applied, the artist sets down his impression of land and sea. We marvel at the effective representation of space, partially achieved by the skillful juxtaposition of darker and lighter planes.

ALBERT MARQUET · THE BEACH AT FéCAMP

Moorland Ditch

Mother and Child with Red Flowers

PAULA MODERSOHN-BECKER · 1876—1907

Paula Modersohn-Becker, all of whose work was painted between 1901 and 1907, heightened a natural lyricism into something approaching the Expressionism of *Die Brücke* (The Bridge). Her desire to depict a romantic, emotional view of nature and the down-to-earth existence of simple rustic people was reinforced by her encounter with Cézanne, Gauguin and the French Symbolists. Her hallmarks are expressive use of color, rigorous stylization of form, which is stripped down to essentials, and a dedication to showing existence in its timelessness, as well as to laying bare the inmost nature of people and things. Her subjects, chiefly flowers and people, are pervaded by a feminine, maternal gentleness. They become true symbols, devoid of narrative content, embodying a solemn, almost monumental existence yet still communicating sensitivity and intuition.

SELF-PORTRAIT WITH CAMELLIA TWIG
1907 · Oil · 24³/₁₆ x 11³/₄ inches · Folkwang Museum, Essen

Paula Modersohn-Becker often painted herself, and this is the last self-portrait she made. The physical subject is concisely summarized. It has lost its depth and lives wholly in the two-dimensionality of the picture plane. The artist, intensifying the expressive quality by use of the narrow format, evokes one person and her feelings. She places the face, with its quiet archaic smile and its great eyes, whose life seems to come from within, in the part of the picture that is densest in color. The painter seems to have captured exactly the expression she was seeking: the joyful, expectant yet anxious feeling of imminent motherhood. The camellia twig held over the chest in a sketchily indicated hand symbolically suggests life to come.

PAULA MODERSOHN-BECKER · SELF-PORTRAIT
WITH CAMELLIA TWIG

At the Edge of the Forest

Vase of Flowers

HENRI ROUSSEAU · 1844—1910

Henri Rousseau, one of the most curious and appealing figures in late nineteenth- and early twentieth-century painting, was the son of a tinsmith. Almost nothing is known about the first thirty years of his life; hearsay claimed that he took part in the French military expedition to Mexico and remained there from 1862 to 1867, and the strong exotic element in his painting was thought to support this. We know that until about 1880 he was a customs official (hence his nickname "Le Douanier"); that he began to paint in the early 1880's, exhibited for the first time in 1885 at the Salon des Champs-Élysées, and in 1886 gave up his job in the Customs to devote himself to art. His artistic vision was so original that it brought him nothing but derision throughout most of his lifetime. Not until shortly before his death did he begin to sell paintings and receive commissions—partly as a result of the respect artists such as Picasso showed for him.

His works, which his contemporaries took for the childish daubs of a selftaught Sunday painter, have been radically reappraised since then. With a genuinely naive primitivism Rousseau evokes a world on the very day of creation, a fantastic, exotic realm of being. This is the spirit which, at the end of the nineteenth century, began to shake the validity of hitherto accepted ideas, which led Van Gogh to become an advocate of emotional expression and drove Gauguin to flee civilization and share the life of natives. It arose out of a desire to break the bonds of reality and attain a new manmade truth, created from within, uncorroded by civilization. Rousseau threw all the resources of his simple, good-natured personality into creating a new pictorial representation reflecting this desire. Untroubled by problems of perspective and the natural appearance of things, he created a reality of objects which are complete in themselves, lovingly and ingenuously distilled out of all their characteristic natural details. A tree, for instance, is represented as a mass of branches with leaves attached to them, a patch of grass is the sum of all the individual blades and tufts. By interweaving minute details of this kind Rousseau allowed his magical universe to spake shape. Other primitive painters used this technique, but none achieved his result.

THE SNAKE CHARMER
1907 · Oil on canvas · 64³/₈ x 72¹/₂ inches · Louvre, Paris

In a dusky primeval landscape built up of innumerable details, the figure of a woman stands by a still, glassy river in the magical light of a full moon. The white highlights of her eyes stare hypnotically out of her silhouetted head, drawing us, like the snakes, into the spell. The white flashes of birds' beaks in the foliage of the jungle trees and of stars glimpsed through the leaves have the same effect. In the foreground sprays of fabulous plants push against the darkness, as though summoned into the light by the strains of the flute, and a fantastic bird stands transfixed. The artist evokes the image of a scene from a far-distant past.

HENRI ROUSSEAU · THE SNAKE CHARMER

Portrieux

Saint Tropez

PAUL SIGNAC · 1836—1935

Paul Signac's parents wanted him to become an architect, but after getting to know the works of Claude Monet in the early 1880's Signac determined to become a painter. In 1884 he began to exhibit with the painters rejected by the jury of the Salon or those who wanted no part in it. Georges Seurat and Henri Edmond Cross became his friends and led him away from Impressionism. Under the influence of Seurat he adopted the Pointillist style of dots of pure, unmixed color that he was to stick to all his life, developing it early in the 1890's into a sort of mosaic of rectangular touches of paint. His favorite subjects were coastal landscapes. He loved the sea and knew many of its shores. In 1888 he explored the Mediterranean coast around Collioure; in 1892 he went sailing on the Atlantic and also discovered Saint Tropez, where he built himself a house he called "The Masthead" as a refuge from Paris. Signac had scholarly interests too and became the theoretician of Pointillism, also called Neo-Impressionism. His book *D'Eugène Delacroix au Néo-Impressionisme,* published in 1899, describes its techniques and development.

PIAZZA DELLA ERBE IN VERONA
1908 · Oil on canvas · 17¹/₂ x 25 inches · Private Collection

Constructed like a mosaic out of tiny squares of paint in very few shades of very few colors, this sun-drenched picture contains the essence of Signac and shows how close he was to Impressionism. We hardly notice that the colors blend in the eye of the viewer rather than on the canvas—as the principles of Pointillism required. And we have to look twice to realize how little the atmosphere of this lively market scene derives from reality and how much of it is created by color—unlike the true Impressionist vision. The sweet note produced by the blending of blue and red into violet is often found in Signac.

PAUL SIGNAC · PIAZZA DELLA ERBE IN VERONA

Javanese Shawl

Rising Sun

MAX PECHSTEIN · 1881—1955

Pechstein was born in Eckersbach near Zwickau. He was apprenticed to a house painter and later attended the Kunstgewerbeschule and the Academy in Dresden. In 1906 he became an Expressionist and a member of *Die Brücke* along with Ernst Ludwig Kirchner, Erich Heckel, Karl Schmidt-Rottluff, and Otto Müller. From the first, however, he held aloof from the revolutionary side of his friends' work, its strident, provocative colors and expression. Although he was commited to expressive art, his style tended to be gentler, his colors more melodious, and because of this he was recognized earlier than the other members of *Die Brücke*. In 1910 he founded the *Neue Sezession* in Berlin, where he lived until his death, except for a period of war service from 1916 to 1917 and five years in Pomerania between 1940 and 1945. He also taught at the Hochschule für Bildende Künste in Berlin.

YOUNG GIRL

1908 · Oil on canvas · 25¹/₂ x 19⁵/₈ inches · Galerie des 20. Jahrhunderts, Berlin

This portrait, painted in rapid, dry strokes of mat, pastellike colors, is a good illustration of Pechstein's brand of Expressionism. Its imitative element is slight and its color is anything but naturalistic, yet it completely lacks the turbulent, shocking vehemence of Heckel, Schmidt-Rottluff or Nolde. The slightly plump young girl delights in her carefree, friendly life—which is the real subject of the painting. The harmonious colors, recalling the *belle peinture* of the Fauves, are well suited to convey this mood.

MAX PECHSTEIN · YOUNG GIRL

Still Day by the Sea III   *Caravels*

LYONEL FEININGER · 1871—1956

Lyonel Feininger was born and died in New York. From his German-born parents he inherited a remarkable musical talent; he was giving public violin recitals when he was twelve. He also composed, and in 1887 went to Hamburg to study music. But painting and drawing interested him more, and he studied art in Hamburg, Berlin and Paris until 1893, when he became a satirical cartoonist for the Berlin journals *Ulk* and *Lustige Blätter*. In 1906 he joined the *Chicago Sunday Tribune* in Paris, but returned to Berlin in 1908 and began to paint.

The milestones that mark Feininger's progress toward his own unmistakable style were his encounter with Cubism and Robert Delaunay's Orphism in 1911 and with the *Blaue Reiter* group in 1913, and above all his invitation to the Bauhaus in Weimar in 1919. Although he adopted Cubism's analytical "fanning-out" of forms and its architectural structural methods, his style stands apart from Cubism. His subjects, usually city scenes and landscapes, were stripped of all local, non-essential elements. Physical things were first reduced to their essential forms, then built into crystalline structures from an architecture of seemingly transparent color planes. His delicately colored paintings, which look almost as if they were composed of stacked sheets of glass, have a strong musical element.

THE GREEN BRIDGE
1909 · Oil on canvas · 39 x 31³/₁₆ inches · Private Collection

This street scene at night shows Feininger as a beginner. The satirical point of view of the cartoonist is still much in evidence. Shady-looking figures slink about the street, and red lights promise surreptitious pleasures. Among the figures is a priest, shepherd of these lost sheep. Like a bridge of honest integrity, the high, un-naturally green arch satirically spans this back-street world, as though reflecting the attitude of the people walking on top of it, who think themselves far above what is going on at their feet. The flatness of the unmodeled color complexes and the unreality of the violets and greens anticipate Feininger's later style.

LYONEL FEININGER · THE GREEN BRIDGE

Composition 8   Angular Construction

WASSILY KANDINSKY · 1866—1944

Kandinsky was born in Moscow, spent his childhood there and in Odessa and when he was nineteen began to study law and economics in Moscow. He did so well that in 1896 he was offered a professorship at the University of Dorpat. He declined because he had just decided to pursue a career in painting, previously only a hobby. He spent two years at the Azbé School in Munich, at that time a center for many young Russians, and got to know his countryman Alexei von Jawlensky. The years from 1896 to 1908 were a time of artistic uncertainty. He attended the Munich Academy, studied under Franz Stuck, taught a little, and traveled widely. His early paintings and woodcuts show the influence of Art Nouveau, late Impressionism and the strong colors of Russian folk art. From 1908 to 1912 Kandinsky spent his summers in Murnau in Bavaria, digesting his travel impressions and painting (chiefly landscapes) in a Fauve yet also very Expressionist style of radically simplified forms and non-representational colors. In 1910 his work became more abstract, and he produced what may be the first non-objective painting, a water color. In 1909 Kandinsky, Jawlensky, Marianne von Werefkin, Adolf Erbslöh, Alexander Kanoldt, and others had founded the *Neue Künstlervereinigung*, but in 1911, as a result of internal dissension over artistic questions, Kandinsky and Franz Marc broke away from it to found the *Blaue Reiter*, which Paul Klee and August Macke joined.

In 1912 Kandinsky published his epochal book *Concerning the Spiritual in Art,* which he had been working on since 1910. This artistic manifesto was followed in 1926 by *Point and Line to Plane,* a basic theoretical work. In painting he consistently followed the abstract direction he had taken in 1910. At first he did not realize that this was a new kind of painting, divorced from experience and significant in itself. This is clear from his own account of an incident that led to a breakthrough. Entering his studio one evening when it was almost dark, instead of a room full of objects he saw "an indescribably beautiful picture, composed of forms and colors, bathed in an inward glow." The next day this picture, which had existed only in his mind's eye, was gone, and he suddenly knew beyond all doubt that real things were harmful to his paintings. From then until World War I, which took him back to Russia until 1922, physical reality began to disappear from his work, which consisted of improvisations, impressions, and resonant color compositions, until finally no trace of it remained.

In 1922 Kandinsky returned to Germany and was appointed to the famous school the Bauhaus, where he remained until 1933. Political events then drove him into exile in Paris, and he died there in 1944. During his last twenty years his style underwent several changes. At first it was geometrical and constructive, in the spirit of *Point and Line to Plane.* In France it acquired a Baroque rhythm and complexity, without losing its tectonic quality, and ultimately it became symbolic, with a monumental cast.

RAILWAY NEAR MURNAU
1909 · Oil on canvas · 14 x 19¹/₈ inches · Städtische Galerie, Munich

The lively colors of this painting from Kandinsky's Murnau days are typical of his first period when he was close to the Fauves. Many details already suggest the transition to the non-representational style the painter was to adopt the following year. We need only look at the top right-hand corner, at the clouds, trees, bushes and meadows translated into sheer color experience. One more small step, and abstract shapes will completely dominate representational forms.

WASSILY KANDINSKY · RAILWAY NEAR MURNAU

Madame Gaudibert   *Hotel de la Plage*

CLAUDE MONET · 1840—1926

On November 14, 1840, Claude Monet was born in Paris. His name has come to stand even more definitively than those of Auguste Renoir, Alfred Sisley, and Camille Pissarro for that special manner of seeing and painting known as Impressionism. It was Monet who, together with his friend Renoir, actually discovered Impressionism and carried this "experiment with light and color" to its logical fulfillment.

Monet grew up in Le Havre and soon showed extraordinary artistic talent, especially in drawing. When he was eighteen Eugène Boudin encouraged him to paint and study from nature. In 1859, after a long struggle with his father who wanted him to go into business, he was allowed to go to Paris for a short period of study, which he managed to prolong by selling signed caricatures. The artists Camille Corot and Charles Daubigny were his models, and he concentrated increasingly on outdoor painting. A long period of military service in Algeria interrupted his development, but in 1862 he began again in Marc Gleyre's studio, where he made friends with his fellow-students Renoir, Frédéric Bazille and Sisley. During the 1860's Monet drew steadily closer to Impressionism as a result of his closeness to nature. His paintings were too revolutionary to bring him recognition or success, and his father refused to support him in what he called his foolishness, so he lived in poverty. Yet material hardship could not distract him from the fanatical pursuit of his goal. During the Franco-Prussian War he spent some time in exile in London, and from 1872 to 1873 lived in Argenteuil on the Seine, where he painted some of his most beautiful pictures, chiefly landscapes, and worked with his friends Manet, Renoir and Sisley. A view of Le Havre entitled "Impression—Sunrise," exhibited at the Impressionists' first group show in 1874, exemplified all the characteristics of this new school of painting and was singled out for attack by the hostile critics—whence the derogatory name "Impressionism."

By 1883 Monet had become known, although he was still far from successful. He moved into a house at Giverny where he was to live an increasingly solitary life until he died. Around the turn of the century he began to work in thicker color and larger planes, but his real theme was still light. Hints began to appear of a style going beyond Impressionism into the visionary and the expressive, especially in his famous water lily paintings, but Monet never pursued these tendencies. He lived on until 1926, aware of having been part of the beginnings of modern art. Today he is admired as one of the most beguiling of painters.

LES DEUX ÉTOILES (detail)
1910 · Oil · 79¹/₂ x 169¹/₄ inches · Collection E. Bührle, Zürich

Monet's late water lily paintings suggest that quite unconsciously and instinctively he had arrived at a style which was still essentially Impressionist and yet close to the aims of the true modern painters. The water lilies stand out as two patches of brilliant light against the rhythmically circling leaves and the expanse of violet-green water that fills the picture space. Monet is not merely describing an optical phenomenon; he is trying in a completely modern way to show the rhythm of forms and color planes.

CLAUDE MONET · LES DEUX ÉTOILES (detail)

Sainte Marguerite in Paris

Gladioluses and Lilies in a Blue Jug

MAURICE UTRILLO · 1883—1955

Utrillo, born out of wedlock to the painter Suzanne Valadon in Paris in 1883, is not one of the great trend-setting pioneers of modern painting but almost an outsider—though an attractive one so far as his work is concerned. From his mother he inherited a genuine natural talent for art, from his father, a clerk by the name of Boissy, a tendency to alcoholism. Even as a boy Utrillo drank excessively; at eighteen he spent a short period—the first of many—in an institution. His mother encouraged him to paint to divert him from drinking, and until about 1907 he worked assiduously but without much conviction, following some unconscious, primitive instinct rather than any particular school. The works of this so-called Montmartre period consist chiefly of views of the suburbs, canyonlike streets and *quais* of Paris and are painted in deep tones of dark colors, thickly applied. They have the honesty and simplicity of Henri Rousseau and an expressive quality that springs straight from the unconscious, uninhibited by the intellect. In the year 1904 alone he painted almost a hundred and fifty pictures of this kind, which for truth and beauty match anything he ever did. We are never aware of the ugliness of the back streets and dirty

walls—and indeed Utrillo never meant to bring out this aspect of a milieu in which he was quite at home.

In 1907 or 1908 his palette began to get lighter, perhaps under the influence of Impressionism, and his paintings, though unchanged in theme, acquired a new freshness, a lightness and luminosity which came from his use of white. This so-called white period lasted until World War I. The almost Impressionist beauty and enamellike luster of the paintings of this period are unmarred by the extraordinary mixtures of white pigment, plaster, glue and ground eggshells that went into them. Probably Utrillo's travels in Corsica and Brittany contributed to the change.

Utrillo was not trying to represent nature in an Impressionist way, however. This is obvious from the curious lack of atmosphere and the substantial solidity of physical objects in his paintings and also by the fact that he liked to work from postcards rather than nature. After World War I, especially in the years around 1927, he adopted a brighter, more pleasing range of colors. He was still enormously productive, but the work he did in the first two decades of the century is unquestionably his best.

MONTMARTRE
1910 · Oil · 10⅞ x 18 inches · Wallraf-Richartz Museum, Cologne

Utrillo captured in this picture a sunny idyll of Montmartre with trees in leaf, strolling people, typical buildings, including a restaurant with its notice that it dispenses *Vins et Liqueurs,* all under a light-filled sky. The scene freezes a moment on a day in a time and in a Montmartre long gone by. The work characterizes the directness

of Utrillo's approach to art, closely derived from the actual scene in nature and devoid of the sophistications of the Fauves and Cubists and other avant-garde artists. At the same time, speaking in his unassuming voice, Utrillo by his individuality and authority marks himself an artist.

MAURICE UTRILLO · MONTMARTRE

Eiffel Tower

Homage to Blériot

ROBERT DELAUNAY · 1885—1941

Robert Delaunay was a native Parisian and received his elementary training in painting at an art school in Belleville. His early works, chiefly portraits and Breton landscapes, are in the Pointillist style of Georges Seurat and Paul Signac. It was no accident that he encountered the work of Cézanne about the same time as did Picasso and Braque, the founders of Cubism. But his deeply poetic nature and inexhaustible passion for color prevented him from whole-heartedly adopting the discreet monochromatic colors and intellectually disciplined architecture of Cubist painting, although his work just before 1910 shows distinct traces of both. He said himself that he wanted to make visible not things but "man's own heartbeat." His aim was color; he wanted to transform the visible into lyrical sound-visions pervaded by rhythmical, dynamic color harmonies. Between 1910 and 1913, when he was approaching his goal, his favorite subjects were sports scenes, churches and, time

and time again, the Eiffel Tower, painted not for their banal reality but for the feeling of action that emanates from athletic events or skyward-reaching towers. To translate this action, as well as the optical experience, into orchestrated color which would communicate emotion through its immediate visual impact was Delaunay's one and only aim. This is what the poet Apollinaire called the Orphic element in his painting. It is not surprising that in 1912—two years later than Kandinsky but quite independently of him—Delaunay should have created a completely non-objective picture—a painting of pure resonance, referring back to nothing but the autonomous, evocative power of color.

Delaunay lived in Spain and Portugal from 1914 to 1920, then he returned to Paris to paint indefatigably until his death in 1941. Though his style changed, he never departed from the delightful luminosity of color he had achieved thirty years earlier.

THE SIMULTANEOUS WINDOWS
1911 · Oil on canvas · 18 x 15⅝ inches · Kunsthalle, Hamburg

Although the explicitly drawn "frame" suggests the windows of the title, and the silhouette thrusting upward in the center of the picture recalls the shape of the Eiffel Tower, we do not need to be told that this is not a specific window or a specific view from any window. The visionary mood of this glimpse of a poetically perceived world has become a pure color experience, communicated through a fine network of geometrical forms (mostly rectangles and triangles) reminiscent of Cézanne and Cubism. Disembodied and ethereal, this mood permeates the "window frame," drawing it into the

rhythmic play of the translucent, harmonizing tones of yellow, green, blue, violet, and orange, from which a mysterious light emanates. Yet at the same time, in an imaginary space existing beyond the movement suggested by the color harmonies themselves, this melodious world of color is pervaded by a strongly felt dynamism climaxing in the arrow of the green "Eiffel Tower." On account of the Eiffel Tower image, an equally suitable title for this painting might be "Paris." But the real subject is the colors and shapes utilized by the artist.

ROBERT DELAUNAY · THE SIMULTANEOUS WINDOWS

Animated Landscape: Man with a Dog

Blue Bottle and Plant

FERNAND LÉGER · 1881—1955

Fernand Léger was born in Argentan in Normandy. In 1897 he was apprenticed to an architect and from 1900 to 1902 he worked as an architectural draftsman in Paris. Because he had to earn his living his real love, painting, could be only a hobby. Nevertheless he experimented with the Impressionist and Pointillist styles, adopted new ideas from Fauvism and finally discovered Cézanne. This encounter led him to a style which brought him close to the Cubists. About 1910 he began to be known and attracted the attention and support of the art dealer Daniel-Henry Kahnweiler.

Léger's aims, already indicated in drawings made between 1906 and 1908, were to use the medium of painting to create a new reality. Not that he rejected the visible, as Kandinsky was doing at about this time. Léger retained externals, but only their outwardness mattered to him, their existence as forms purified of all illusion and contingency, which could provide him, so to speak, with depersonalized architectural blocks for constructing his pictures. He combined "natural" forms of this kind with imaginative "art" forms, organizing them according to the laws of color, with a disciplined, clear structuring of all formal elements. Thus even before World War I he had created an idiom purged of the irrelevant, in which nothing was left to chance. The forms assembled on the canvas were by no means just a dead conglomeration. To Léger natural things were not lifeless organisms. Like the scientists, he saw them as constantly moving, living entities made up of tiny units, and he believed that the painting should also reflect a dynamic motion.

It was almost to be expected that between 1916 and 1920 Léger should discover the world of technology and machines, the beauty of lucid industrial form and energy. He painted human figures constructed of basic geometrical elements: cones, spheres and cylinders. In poster design, carpet and tapestry weaving and commercial art Léger also set new trends. He died at Gif-sur-Yvette in 1955, having pursued his aims with unusual consistency throughout his lifetime.

STUDY FOR THE "WOMAN IN BLUE"
1912 · Oil · 75⅝ x 50¾ inches · Kunstmuseum, Basel

This picture of a seated woman is Cubist in construction inasmuch as it is not subject to natural perspective and illumination, but unlike early Cubist paintings it relies on the effect of rich colors. If we look closely we can distinguish the essential parts of the woman's body: the head, with the face in profile, the neck, shoulders, arms and hands, the legs turned sideways. We also discover fragments of her physical surroundings: tabletops and legs, a pair of scissors, a glass. We can also see the Cubistically dissected figure resolving itself into mechanical forms. The metallic implications of the blue seem to place it in the manmade world of machines.

102

FERNAND LÉGER · STUDY FOR THE "WOMAN IN BLUE"

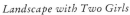
Landscape with Two Girls

Market in Tunis I

AUGUST MACKE · 1887—1914

Macke was born in Meschede, Westphalia. Killed at the age of twenty-seven in the early days of World War I, he was not destined to realize his full potential as an artist. After studying at the Dusseldorf Academy and Kunstgewerbeschule, he joined the avant-garde, first in Paris in 1907 and then as one of the supporters of the *Blaue Reiter* in Munich. He was serene and cheerful by disposition and remained more committed to reality than his associates. He was attracted by the colorful diversity of life, by all that went on in the streets, parks and cafés, by the intimate world of shop windows. His unproblematical oil paintings and water colors reflect joy of living; their glowing color recalls the Fauves—for color, much more than form, was Macke's forte. Franz Marc in a eulogy of his friend expressed what color meant to Macke: "We painters know well that with the passing of his harmony, color in German art will become several shades paler and its timbre will grow duller and drier. He, more than any of us, gave color its clearest, purest resonance—clear and pure as his whole life." The inspiration of these meaningful words may be observed in his canvases.

THE ARTIST'S WIFE
1912 · Oil · 41 x 31½ inches · Galerie des 20. Jahrhunderts, Berlin

Elisabeth Gerhardt, whom Macke married in 1909, was a favorite subject, but his paintings of her usually are not portraits. Generally she is engaged in some activity: knitting, enjoying the garden or a book, as she is in this picture where Macke's real theme is the quiet absorption of reading. He depicts it through big areas of clear colors, outlined by beautifully flowing lines, cool but not cold in mood. Darkness balances lightness; the silence of the room is perfectly captured; the emphasis is on the counterpoise of open book and bent head. The skillful use of color and form captures a feeling of deep tranquillity.

AUGUST MACKE · THE ARTIST'S WIFE

Dancer at the Bal Tabarin   *Mosaic*

GINO SEVERINI · 1883—1966

Gino Severini, who was born in Tuscany, at Cortona, went to Rome to study in 1901. By 1906 he had made many close friends in Paris among artists and was exchanging ideas with Amedeo Modigliani, Maurice Utrillo, Raoul Dufy, and Georges Braque. His marriage to the daughter of the eminent French poet Paul Fort in 1913 gave him entrée to intellectual circles too. In 1910 his dissatisfaction with Cubism's static architectonics and restrained colors led him to join some like-minded fellow-Italians including Umberto Boccioni, Giacomo Balla and Luigi Russolo in signing the First Manifesto of Futurist Painters. Severini became one of the most distinctive representatives of Futurism and its only representative in France. He stayed with this movement until 1915 and painted several pictures which excellently achieve the purpose of conveying the sensation of movement by splitting up the subject into multiple individual views and showing them all simultaneously on the canvas. Next came a phase of consolidation, bringing him closer to Cubism, which in the meantime had given up its asceticism and been converted to color (in no small degree through Severini's own influence). About 1920 his clear mathematical mind began to seek a new classical form retaining the rules of proportion and a kind of painting in which physical objects, stripped down to their classic form, could again play a part. His book *Du Cubisme au Classicisme* (1921) discusses these new aims. His later works, predominantly still lifes, are clearer in conception, reflecting the wisdom of old age, but for all of this they are no less expressive than his earlier paintings.

AUTOBUS
1912 · Oil on canvas · 10⁷/₈ x 7⁷/₈ inches · Private Collection

This small picture is obviously an attempt to combine the stability of Cubism with the dynamics of Futurism. Planes and scrolls which seem motionless when looked at individually are drawn by the swirling curves into a movement intended to convey the sensation of going somewhere, rolling along, flashing by. The crinkled white patterns introduce a sense of shaking, of a vehicle clattering along.

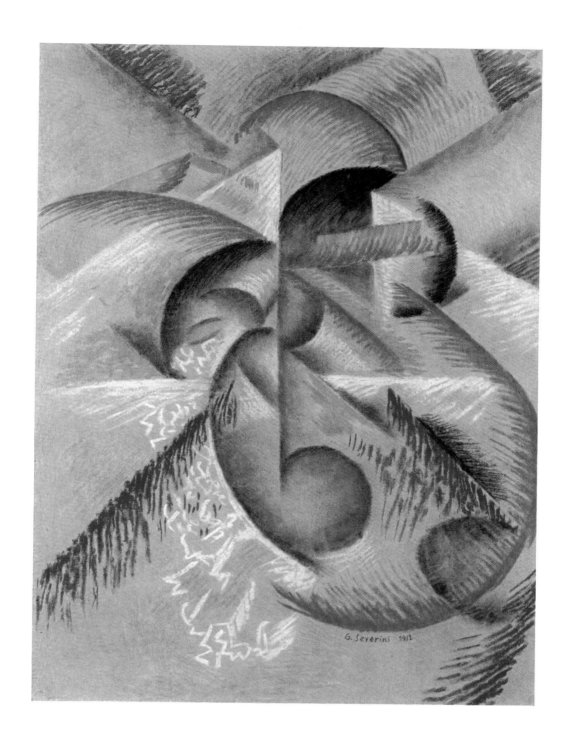

GINO SEVERINI · AUTOBUS

Tillya

Girl with Blue Eyes

MARIE LAURENCIN · 1885—1956

Marie Laurencin was one of the few women to fight in the front lines of modernism; she upheld its aims not only in her own painting but through other activities too. One of these was the journal called "391" which she, Francis Picabia, Albert Gleizes, and Arthur Cravan founded in Barcelona in 1917 to promote modern art. Marie Laurencin first attracted attention in the exhibition of the *Section d'Or* group in 1912. She was close to Cubism artistically, although she never joined this strongly intellectual movement. One might say that she had a brief encounter with it and adopted certain things from it, but essentially she remained committed to a more or less pronounced realism which never lost touch with nature. About 1918, after her semi-Cubist phase, this realism became more dominant and gave her work an appealing charm, which is especially effective in her portraits of women.

THE POETESS
1912 · Oil on canvas · 32 x 25³/₈ inches · Private Collection

The subject is probably Marguerite Gillot, a friend of Apollinaire and Paul Fort and a member of Picasso's early circle. Although the monochromatic colors and fragmentation of objects recall Cubism, the slim, longnecked woman with her strangely fascinating almond eyes suggests Modigliani rather than the contemporary works of Picasso or Braque. Marie Laurencin is not trying to depict her subject by representing it from all angles simultaneously, as Cubist laws prescribe; she is trying to reproduce feminine beauty and grace—reduced to its simplest forms, to be sure, and caught in a beautiful play of curving lines.

MARIE LAURENCIN · THE POETESS

The Red Deer II

Two Horses in the Landscape

FRANZ MARC · 1880—1916

When Franz Marc was killed at Verdun in March, 1916, modern painting, still in its infancy, lost one of its most outstanding and attractive talents. Marc began as a student of theology and philosophy but soon discovered that painting was his real calling. He began to find himself about 1907 or 1908 while he was still working in an Impressionist style. In words that pointed to the direction his future work would take, he once said that an inner voice had told him to "go back to nature; go back to the utmost simplicity, for there alone lies the symbolism, the pathos and the mystery of nature. Everything else distracts, diminishes, produces discord." Stimulated by his fellow-members of the *Blaue Reiter* Wassily Kandinsky, August Macke and Paul Klee, he began in 1910 to translate into painting the essential principles he had already recognized intellectually. His aim was "to create symbols of the age for the altars of the spiritual religion to come." His theme was animals, which he saw as pure, uncorrupted Creation—for his painting was sustained by a profound and genuinely religious emotion. In resonant chords of non-representational colors and in rhythmically organized swinging forms Marc conveys the animal's own self-awareness in its creaturely existence. This feeling persists in the pictures he painted about 1912. Here, under the influence of Cubism and Futurism, the form became less fluid and the picture space fragmented into jagged, furrowlike shapes. Marc's powerful, dynamically moving color gives these works an expressiveness he had never attained before. At the end of his life Marc was reaching toward pure color orchestrations and formal compositions, but he had no chance to develop these to the mastery achieved in his earlier animal works.

TWO HORSES
About 1912—1913 · Oil on canvas · 15³/₈ x 13 inches · Rhode Island Institute of Design, Providence

Two horses, condensed into a formal symbol for "horse," exist in a picture-space constructed of color planes broken up into what look like facets. The animals' bodies are inextricably interlinked with these shapes, as revealed in the diagonals formed by the spine of the horse in the foreground and the rays of light breaking in from the top right-hand corner. They give the total picture an extraordinary stillness, concentrated in its center, which overpowers even the vertical thrust of the animals' crowding bodies and the dynamic upward accent of their colors. The whole existential world of these animals is translated into color and form. We can actually feel the still horse, painted in warm reds in a setting of brighter planes, abandoning itself to the invigorating warmth of the sunbeams. The blue horse is quite different. His raised head and pricked ears create a feeling of alertness. He belongs to the world of night, suggested by its symbols of moon and stars, and by the cool tones of blue and green.

FRANZ MARC · TWO HORSES

Birds and Oceans

Old Man River — Vater Rhein

MAX ERNST · 1891—

Max Ernst was born in Brühl near Cologne. He studied philosophy at the University of Bonn and began to paint after he graduated, about 1913. From the outset he was drawn to Surrealism and by the 1920's had become its outstanding representative. He supported the ideas of the Dada movement established in Zurich in 1916, and with Hans Arp and Alfred Grünewald (I. T. Baargeld) founded its German school in Cologne in 1919. Dada was an international revolt against the validity of the world seemingly authenticated by logic and reason. Born of spiritual uncertainty and the relativization of all values, it was fostered by World War I. It aimed at bringing to light from man's unconscious and his dreams insights that would be more real and true than those of the everyday world, whose narrow-minded cocksureness and existence Dada took a truly macabre pleasure in questioning and declaring bankrupt. Ernst and some fellow-painters, including Joan Miró and Salvador Dali, were determined to get rid of everything logical and to bring the stuff of dreams, the nonsensical, the parapsychological, into play. They wanted to present the magical, the fantastic and the unreal and use it to ridicule the visible and also to open up new areas of experience, and they developed an art of the surreal in which the impossible becomes possible. Human, animal and vegetable things, meaningless in themselves, entered into a fantastic symbiosis in which the gruesome and the comic are equally at home and whose abstruse forms, often depicted with meticulous fidelity, offer the associative mind infinite scope.

Ernst once said that his aim was "to capture the optical hallucination with the utmost precision." To stress the unreality of his pictures, which are really not pictures at all in the true sense, he often used unusual techniques such as *frottage* (rubbings) and *collage* (paste-up). He has also done frescoes, stage sets and sculpture. Ernst lived in Paris from 1922 until 1941, when he went to the United States. He returned to Paris in 1949.

TIME OF THE FORESTS
1913 · Oil on canvas · 35¹/₂ x 23³/₈ inches · Private Collection

"Tree" forms, which look liked striped or streaked green posts, crowd together in a dense, somehow threatening mass, as if they were living beings. It is as though the forest were gathering its strength to confront man. Even without the title, association would tell us that the picture has something to do with forests, although the forms look completely unreal.

MAX ERNST · TIME OF THE FORESTS

Oldenburg Landscape

Calla Lily

KARL SCHMIDT-ROTTLUFF · 1884—

Karl Schmidt, who later added the name of his birthplace, Rottluff near Chemnitz, to his name, entered the Dresden Technische Hochschule in 1905 to study architecture. There he met Erich Heckel, a former schoolmate, and Ernst Ludwig Kirchner, with whom he founded *Die Brücke* (The Bridge) that same year. Apart from Emil Nolde he is the only member of that German Expressionist group to have pursued expressive painting consistently throughout his long life. He was also the only one of the former architecture students who retained a constructional element in his work.

After an early Impressionist phase, Schmidt-Rottluff emphasized the structure of his subjects (chiefly landscapes), using strongly contrasting colors. After World War I, in which he served from 1915 to 1918, the architectural elements at times became even more noticeable, especially in his woodcuts, bringing him close to early Cubism. The portraits and figure paintings of this period are monumentally dynamic in line and show a deep, emotional serious-

ness. In 1919 Schmidt-Rottluff settled in Berlin but traveled extensively. Between 1920 and 1927 he turned increasingly to religious themes, and his painting acquired a visionary quality. Human figures and nature were reduced to concise, angular, graphic forms which made them look as if they were carved out of wood, and painted in colors arbitrarily chosen for their expressive effect. In the mid-1920's his style became more representational and remained so, without ever becoming naturalistic or losing its full color resonance.

In 1933 under the Nazi regime Schmidt-Rottluff was expelled from the Akademie der Bildenden Künste in Berlin; in 1937 he was outlawed as a "degenerate artist." Six hundred and eight of his pictures were confiscated. In 1941 he and Nolde were forbidden to paint and subjected to police supervision. In 1946 he joined the faculty of the Berlin Hochschule für Bildende Kunst. His *œuvre* also includes outstanding graphic art and excellent sculpture.

LIGHTHOUSE ON THE BALTIC COAST
1913 · Oil · 29¼ x 34⅞ inches · Private Collection

This landscape and the lighthouse from which the painting gets its title are composed of large color planes painted in quick, broad brushstrokes and bordered with dark lines. The artist seems to have paid little attention to natural light, space or perspective. While

the tree, house, meadow and field, and road classify the painting as a landscape, its essential elements are the resonant harmony of contrasting colors and radically simplified forms. The result is a composition of directness and strength.

KARL SCHMIDT-ROTTLUFF · LIGHTHOUSE ON THE
BALTIC COAST

Still Life with Ginger Pot

Gray Tree

PIET MONDRIAN · 1872—1944

Even as a boy Piet Mondrian was, as he said, "possessed by the demon of painting." To please his father, an elementary school teacher in Amersfoort, he took up teaching, but later, despite his parents' objections, exchanged this safe profession for an artist's freedom and the material insecurity that goes with it. He attended the Amsterdam Academy from 1892 to 1895, then spent two years taking advanced courses. He earned his living by making copies of seventeenth-century masters for rich art-lovers, acquiring technical skill in the process. About 1905 the competent, academic straightforwardness of his early paintings, which were chiefly landscapes, began to give way to Pointillist experiment. At this time he took up theosophy, a subject which occupied him for decades, and his painting sometimes strikes a symbolic note.

In 1911 Mondrian saw his first Cubist paintings; they more than anything else stimulated him to develop the personal style which consistently sought to create an abstract picture entirely free of representation. In 1911 he went to Paris, returning to Holland in 1914. Supported by Theo van Doesburg of the journal *De Stijl*, whose aims were similar, he began about 1920 to acquire his own manner, which he stuck to and constantly refined until his death in New York in 1944. He was continually pressing toward pure abstraction until in the end the vocabulary of his painting consisted exclusively of rectangular planes of unmixed basic colors (red, blue, yellow and white, with black and gray) and rectangular patterns made by the intersecting of straight vertical and horizontal lines of varying thickness.

COMPOSITION IN OVAL
1914 · Oil · 44 x 33 inches · Gemeente Museum, The Hague

Like many comparable works painted about 1915, this picture marks Mondrian's transition from Cubism to a purely abstract style. The network (here still a broken one) of largely horizontal and vertical lines and the method of constructing the picture out of areas of color (pink, ocher, blue and grayish tones) indicate what is to come, although this work does not approach the strength and purity Mondrian was later to achieve. Nature is still too close—and Cubism too, which always took natural objects as its point of departure. This picture really belongs to the series of

church facades and seascapes that Mondrian painted at this time. The following quotation from *Toward the True Vision of Reality* (1942) explains what he was trying to do: "I would look at the sea, the sky and the stars and represent it all by a lot of crosses. I was impressed by the greatness of nature and I was trying to express the vastness of space, peace and unity. Yet I felt I was still working as an Impressionist, expressing a specific, limited experience but not reality as it actually is." This statement reflects Mondrian's philosophical orientation toward art.

PIET MONDRIAN · COMPOSITION IN OVAL

The Champagne Song (detail)   *The Spanish Dancer—Marietta di Rigardo*

MAX SLEVOGT · 1868—1932

Max Slevogt, a native of Landshut, was a Bavarian of the old school. His training and development were similar to Max Liebermann's. While he never encountered socially critical painting such as that of Jean Millet, he too was decisively influenced by Dutch painting. He admired Rembrandt, perhaps because Rembrandt appealed to his taste for dramatic gesture—for Slevogt was a devotee of the theater all his life. Under the influence of the Dutch *plein air* movement he soon broke away from hidebound studio painting. He moved to Berlin in 1901 and together with Lieber-mann and Lovis Corinth became a follower of Impressionism. The numerous pictures he painted in a year-long visit to Egypt in 1913 demonstrate at its most appealing (though not necessarily at its best) his unrivaled gift for portraying in fresh colors, applied in rapid, fluent strokes, a serene world to which he sometimes gives a theatrical intensity. The brilliant, light-drenched color effects he achieved under the African sun can compete with French Impressionism at its best. With his innate love of story-telling, Slevogt used his mastery of color to depict scenes real and imaginary.

PIRATES
1914 · Oil · 28½ x 37 inches · Staatliche Gemäldegalerie, Dresden

One notes the shimmering water and sky, the scene captured in fluid strokes of thick paint. Slevogt's enthusiasm for the dramatic is perfectly reflected in his flamboyant handling of the pigment. A sense of motion is engendered by the diagonal lines of the oar and mast, and by the leaning posture of the oarsmen, sketched in broadest forms.

MAX SLEVOGT · PIRATES

The Picnic Grounds
1906/07 · Oil on canvas · 24 x 36 inches ·
Collection Whitney Museum
of American Art, New York

Sixth Avenue Elevated at Third Street
1928 · Oil on canvas · 30 x 40 inches ·
Collection Whitney Museum
of American Art, New York

JOHN SLOAN · 1871—1951

John Sloan, a prominent member of the Philadelphia group that revolutionized American art in the early years of the twentieth century, was born in 1871 in Lock Haven, Pennsylvania. Some years later his family moved to Philadelphia, where he was reared. His stupendous gift for drawing was revealed early, and he taught himself to etch when he was seventeen. Sloan started his career as illustrator for two Philadelphia newspapers, the *Enquirer* and then the *Press*. He also attended an evening class at the Pennsylvania Academy of Fine Art, where the students drew from casts. Dissatisfied, he formed a short-lived group, The Charcoal Club, whose members hired a model and obtained Robert Henri, six years Sloan's senior, to give criticism. To Henri, who stressed the importance of life as the primary motive of art, Sloan owed his development away from academic idealism toward realism.

In 1905 Sloan, then newly married, moved to New York. He had already begun to paint, inspired by the street life of Philadelphia, but now he waxed enthusiastic about New York with its teeming crowds of various types of people. Though he continued to earn his living as an illustrator, he devoted more time to painting. When a canvas by his friend George Luks was rejected by the conservative National Academy in New York, the two men, seeking support for their progressive ideas, formed a group with Arthur B. Davies, William Glackens, Robert Henri, Ernest Lawson, Maurice Prendergast, and Everett Shinn. They became know as The Eight. Their preferred subject was everyday life, including the slums and the squalor of the metropolis. Unsympathetic colleagues referred to them as the Black Gang and the Ashcan School.

Though encouraged by the more liberal critics, Sloan would have starved without his income as an illustrator. He was forty-two before he sold a painting. In the same year, 1913, his canvas, "Sunday, Girls Drying Their Hair," was hung in the famous Armory Show. Four years later he participated in founding the Society of Independent Artists. He also demonstrated his defiance by joining the Socialist Party and making illustrations for its magazine, "The Masses." Nevertheless, he found an ardent sponsor in a millionaire's daughter, Gertrude Vanderbilt Whitney, who exhibited his work in her studio (from which the Whitney Museum was to emerge). Slowly, success came and in his final decades Sloan was able to devote himself almost exclusively to painting.

Sloan's early drawings were influenced by the decorative style of Art Nouveau. He changed under the impact of Henri's dark Impressionism, and the masters to whom Henri introduced him. From Goya and Damier he adopted a vigorous, agitated brushwork. Though he admired Renoir and Van Gogh, his own colors remained low-keyed. Recalling, in his old age, his switch to a bold, robust realism, he said that he and his associates had come to it "as a revolt against sentimentality and artificial subject matter and the cult of art for art's sake." He has been called the American Hogarth because he often painted people on sidewalks, in bars, or on the roofs and fire escapes of tenement houses in lower Manhattan. Late in life he made many cross-hatched and glazed studies of the female nude, which along with the landscapes he painted in Gloucester, Massachusetts, and Santa Fé, New Mexico, are highly prized.

BACKYARDS, GREENWICH VILLAGE
1914 · Oil on canvas · 26 x 32 inches · Whitney Museum of American Art, New York

Looking at this picture, one can easily understand why conservative artists and critics were enraged by Sloan's art: there is nothing noble, nothing dignified about the subject matter. By 1914, the Impressionists, with their simple subjects of boating and sailing, meadows and bouquets of flowers, had become acceptable, but there was still no tolerance for "sordid" subjects like this one of the slums.

120

JOHN SLOAN · BACKYARDS, GREENWICH VILLAGE

The Forces of a Street

States of Mind: The Farewells
Collection, The Museum of Modern Art,
New York

UMBERTO BOCCIONI · 1882—1916

Boccioni's name will always be associated with that far-reaching though short-lived phenomenon in modern painting: Futurism. At first he painted in the Impressionist and Pointillist style to which Gino Severini and Giacomo Balla introduced him during his years in Rome between 1898 and 1902. In 1909 he met the poet Filippo Tomasso Marinetti, who had issued a manifesto establishing new aims for literature, and decided to try to formulate equivalent aims for the visual arts. In 1910, together with Carlo Carrà, Luigi Russolo, Balla, and Severini, he issued the "First Manifesto of Futurist Painters" proclaiming the goals of the new movement, which pledged itself to renounce tradition and look to the future. In the few years remaining to him before he was killed in action in 1916, he painted the comprehensive visions of reality that Futurism aspired to. Without rejecting the visible world, they presented a more complex, complete reality than the one that meets the eye, primarily through Boccioni's use of images and color suggestive of physical movement, speed, the passing of time, and even acoustic sensations—a whole range of sensory experience that had never before been expressible in visual terms. This extension of artistic range reflects the aims of Futurism.

UNDER THE PERGOLA IN NAPLES
1914 · Oil · 32³/₈ x 32³/₈ inches · Galleria d'arte moderna, Milan

Even a viewer with no experience in reading modern paintings will immediately recognize what this one represents, despite the Cubist "fanning out" of the motif with little regard for perspective and the restriction of the palette to a few totally unrealistic colors. Against the background of Vesuvius two people are eating a meal—the plate of the man at the right suggests fish—and are drinking red wine. The green carafe is clearly stated, and the unexplained mandolin suggests the sound of string music that is so much a part of the Neapolitan ambiance. At the upper right the corner of a newspaper interjects a startling note of realism—a challenge to see the picture as an object rather than as a representation of a scene.

UMBERTO BOCCIONI · UNDER THE PERGOLA IN NAPLES

House in Soest

Soest

CHRISTIAN ROHLFS · 1849—1938

Christian Rohlfs, born in Niendorf near Leezen in Holstein, was the son of a farmer and all his life he remained close to nature. He was trained in Berlin and Weimar. During the 1880's he came under the spell of Impressionism, which he never entirely rejected, but about the turn of the century he turned to the strongly expressive style associated with Emil Nolde, who became his friend in 1905.

Rohlfs, however, held back, consciously or unconsciously, from the violence of color and form so characteristic of Nolde. Even when his color does strike a strident note, he tempers it with Impressionist effects of light and atmosphere. This gives his paintings, chiefly flower pieces, city landscapes and religious themes, an almost dreamy charm that is unmistakably his own.

THE PRODIGAL SON I
1915 · Oil on canvas · 43 x 29¼ inches · Private Collection

This picture, one of a cycle, is obviously very close to Expressionism, particularly in the way the forms of the prodigal and the two questionable girls accompanying him are condensed into large-scale simplicity. The colors, which recall Otto Müller, are restrained rather than loud, and the tonal values produce a soothing, quite unaggressive feeling.

CHRISTIAN ROHLFS · THE PRODIGAL SON I

Summer
1911 · Gouache on cardboard ·
24¹/₈ x 18¹/₂ inches · Collection
Whitney Museum of American Art,
New York

Adoration of the Moon
1944 · Oil on canvas · 48 x 32 inches ·
Collection Whitney Museum
of American Art, New York

MAX WEBER · 1881—1960

Max Weber was born in Byelostok, Russia, in 1881. When he was ten, his family moved to Brooklyn in New York City. Weber studied at the Pratt Institute, New York, and from 1905 to 1908 he lived in France, for a time attending classes at a school run by Henri Matisse in Paris. After his return to New York City, the photographer and dealer Alfred Stieglitz showed his work at the gallery "291" on Fifth Avenue. From the mid-twenties until his death in 1960 Max Weber lived quietly and frugally in Long Island, New York. For a time he was a teacher with the Art Students League of New York. Fame came to him only in 1949, when the Whitney Museum of American Art held a retrospective exhibit of his paintings.

From Matisse, Weber learned to use flat color set down in pure tone and juxtaposed without transition. From Cézanne, he learned to portray, through the interplay of colorplanes, inner structure rather than external appearance. But while Weber never met Cézanne, he did know Henri Rousseau, the French primitive painter. He admired and adapted Rousseau's simplicity and architectural conciseness, learning how to "edit" nature by heightening significant features and discarding less important ones.

For about a decade after his return form Europe, Weber painted pictures with a growing boldness that resulted in near-abstractions. In rich colors and geometric patterns, he glorified the dynamics of the metropolis. When they were first shown in New York, a critic attacked these works as the emanations of someone not in his right mind, "such as one might expect from the inmate of a lunatic asylum."

After about 1918 Weber produced more representational pictures, works more accessible to those not accustomed to approach a painting as they would music, without concern for subject matter. Weber felt, however, that he had reached the end of near-abstract painting. He thus described his "return" to nature: "In my early days I discovered the geometry in the works of God. Now I felt the need to return to the works of God themselves."

This Expressionist art of the mature Weber overflows with spirituality. His landscapes with trees are somber and melancholy; his still lifes are full of vitality; his plump nudes are unseductive, yet fascinatingly disturbing; his musicians make you hear the music; his sweating workmen struggle with structural steel. Weber frequently painted dynamic Jewish groups, bearded men using eloquent hands to underline an argument or dancing ecstatically before the Lord. He distorted their faces and figures to reach the highest pitch of emotional spiritual experience. His credo is couched in these words:

"The materialist asks of what use are art forms, and the infidel asks of what use is prayer. Both ask the question to which the dumb beasts find answer in the satisfaction of their hunger. Art like faith cannot be explained away. It is the faith found in feeling, the feeling that comes of an art consciousness, the consciousness of spirit inherent in matter."

CHINESE RESTAURANT
1915 · Oil on canvas · 40 x 48 inches · Whitney Museum of American Art, New York

About this chromatic fantasy, from the middle of his "abstract" period, the artist wrote: "On entering a Chinese restaurant from the darkness of the night outside, a maze and blaze of light seemed to split into fragments the interior and its contents . . . The light so piercing and so luminous, the color so liquid and the life and movement so enchanting! To express this, kaleidoscopic means had to be chosen." And indeed they were in this fragmented representation of great refinement.

MAX WEBER · CHINESE RESTAURANT

Still Life with Book

Still Life with Bottle and Glass

JUAN GRIS · 1887—1927

Juan Gris, whose real name was José Gonzáles and who was born in Madrid, began to paint relatively late. He originally intended to become an engineer but was not able to complete his studies, and this early interest may explain why he turned first to drawing. Around the turn of the century and in the years following his move to Paris in 1906, graphic art remained his domain, and he did not really become a painter until about 1910, partly through the influence of his compatriot Picasso, a fellow-tenant of the *Bateau Lavoir,* that dilapidated tenement in the Rue Ravignan. Working in close contact with Picasso and other painters pursuing similar aims, Gris soon found his style: Cubism. Yet from the start his purpose was not to penetrate and dissect the motif but rather to synthesize, to allow objects to take shape through the organization of forms on the canvas. "I turn a cylinder into a bottle," he once said to point up the contrast with Cézanne, who proceeded in the opposite direction: from bottle to cylinder. For Gris the idea came first; the picture was just a means of realizing it, without of course relinquishing all contact with outside reality—except that this reality is brought in by the back door, so to speak. It appears in form elements which are complete in themselves and can be shuffled and rearranged like the letters of the alphabet. Seen in their totality, they invariably spell out "mandolin," "human head," "pitcher," or whatever the idea may be.

Gris was the most logical of all the Cubists; he developed the potentialities of this kind of painting to their limits. He died of toxemia in Paris at the age of forty.

LE PETIT DÉJEUNER
1915 · Oil on canvas · 31⁵/₈ x 25³/₈ inches · Private Collection

This magnificent painting is a fine example of Gris' brand of synthetic Cubism. Color planes of varying hues, some imitating natural materials, others non-representational, are fanned out in close juxtaposition, like cards in a player's hand. The things on the breakfast table are rendered either in outline or in accurate perspective: coffee mill, glass carafe, metal coffee pot, cup, and drinking glass. Although they are broken up into fragments, the sum total of individual views adds up to a still life. We can also identify the table, the paneled wall of the breakfast room and the crisp folds of the tablecloth. This is a painting of highly sophisticated color.

JUAN GRIS · LE PETIT DÉJEUNER

Portrait of an Army Doctor
Solomon R. Guggenheim Museum,
New York

Brooklyn Bridge
Solomon R. Guggenheim Museum,
New York

ALBERT GLEIZES · 1881—1953

Gleizes, the son of a technical draftsman, was born in Paris. He began to paint in an Impressionist style but about 1909 turned to Cubism as created by Picasso and Braque. He had a good theoretical mind, and his book *Du Cubisme,* written in collaboration with Jean Metzinger and published in 1912, made him the spokesman of this branch of modern painting in the early years of the twentieth century. He remained true to Cubism throughout his life, although his association with Robert Delaunay led him to depart more and more from its object-associated constructive principles and pursue rhythm and dynamics through color.

PORTRAIT OF FLORENT SCHMITT
1915 · Oil · 39³/₈ x 39³/₈ inches · Musée National d'Art Moderne, Paris

The cryptic symbols for hand and eye, the rounded forms denoting head and body, prove that this is not entirely a non-representational composition merely trying to convey tonality of color and dynamics of form, but a picture of a specific person, Florent Schmitt. Here, however, the pure Cubist technique of first dissecting the object and then constructing a pictorial entity out of its jagged, fanned-out forms is no longer dominant. Neither is Cubism's constructive form, although angular planes are still used. Through color contrast and the spiral movement of shapes and lines whose vortex is the center of the bearded face, Gleizes has created an extraordinarily vital kind of portrait. One would not call it realistic, yet it has its own verity.

ALBERT GLEIZES · PORTRAIT OF FLORENT SCHMITT

Portrait of the Engraver Gosvel   *Self-Portrait*

AMEDEO MODIGLIANI · 1884—1920

Modigliani's short life, marked by tuberculosis and escape into hashish and alcohol, began in Leghorn in 1884 and ended in the Charité Hospital in Paris in 1920. It was a life that finds little parallel in his art. Forced to drop out of school because of illness, he took up painting as a stimulating recreation and in 1906 went to live in Paris, the artists' Mecca. Poor, plagued by chronic depression, morose rather than sociable, he nevertheless quickly made contact with other painters. Although this close association with artists and writers (interrupted for a year in 1909, when Modigliani returned to Italy) led to no intimate friendships, it was enormously productive and helped him to get off to a meteoric start—artistically, if not financially.

Under the influence of Toulouse-Lautrec and Picasso he soon gave up the realistic style of drawing and painting he had acquired in Italy in favor of large-scale, structured form. This tendency was encouraged by the sculptor Constantin Brancusi under whose guidance Modigliani concentrated on sculpture for a time, and by his encounter with African art. But his strongly sensuous nature and his almost pathological attachment to life prevented him from accepting Cubism's intellectual discipline. He preferred Cézanne's closeness to nature and remained firmly committed to reality all his life, although he never sought merely to reproduce it. When World War I broke out he had already developed his own personal style, a mixture of realism and a poetically transfigured idealism, dictated by his liking for big, statuesque form and expressive line, but pervaded by an undertone of delicate melancholy. This emotion is diffused throughout his portraits, which soon became his favorite subject.

SEATED WOMAN
1918 · Oil · 39 x 25³/₈ inches · Private Collection, Paris

This half-figure, a late work of the short-lived artist, illustrates Modigliani's unique characteristiscs. The figure of a young woman, reduced to its simplest essentials, characteristically elongated and outlined by clear, sweeping lines, exists in a still, silent world from which all non-essentials have been eliminated. Posed against a simple background, which frames it rather than lending it depth, it has an ideal actuality modified by a meditative melancholy. This feeling is strongest in the bright patch of light of the face. The dreamy, opaque eyes and the angle of the head on the long neck sustain it, and the harmonizing colors of the dress and background also make their contribution. The total result is a composition of elegance and a feeling for the model as an individual.

AMEDEO MODIGLIANI · SEATED WOMAN

Woman on a Blue Divan   *Girl's Head with Sunflowers*

ERNST LUDWIG KIRCHNER · 1880—1938

As a child Kirchner showed a strong inclination for drawing and painting which his father, an engineer, encouraged. As an eighteen-year-old high school student at the Germanisches Museum in Nuremberg he was deeply impressed by the graphic art of Albrecht Dürer, and this may well have been the beginning of his never-ending love for woodcuts, etchings and lithographs. He studied architecture at the Dresden Technische Hochschule, and his first attempts at painting and etching date from this time (about 1901). In 1904 he met Erich Heckel, with whom he would later travel a common road. A Pointillist exhibition in Munich stimulated him to continue the process of freeing color from its association with objects, while at the same time the Japanese color prints and the African art he saw in museums prompted him to seek primitive, simple form. Heckel had introduced him to Karl Schmidt-Rottluff, and in 1905 the three of them formed the artists' community known as *Die Brücke* (The Bridge). In 1906 Kirchner, as the group's intellectual leader, wrote its program.

Kirchner broke with tradition completely. Subordinating representational likeness, he turned his pictures into striking compositions made up of big areas of color, slapped explosively on the canvas in furious brushstrokes. This style, which is closely related optically to Fauvism and which often looks sketchy and impulsive, reached its highpoint in the street scenes, the nudes and bathers, and the circus and music-hall motifs of his Berlin period (1911 to 1915). These works have a strangely Gothic jaggedness and awkwardness of form, no doubt inspired by medieval woodcuts, and a restless vibrancy of color; the function of both was to strip away the facade of city life and reveal its internal cleavages.

In 1917, after a brief period of war service which overtaxed him mentally and physically, Kirchner went to live in Switzerland. In this world of peasants and mountains his painting drew closer to nature. Its earlier nervousness was calmed into large forms and color areas which convey the impact of the rugged country with ecstatic yet monumental exuberance. About 1926, after a side-glance at what Picasso was doing at the time, he took a semi-abstract Cubist direction but never entirely negated reality.

Official condemnation of his work and that of his friends after 1933 by the Nazi regime plunged Kirchner into a destructive despair, which was aggravated by a painfull illness. He took his own life in 1938.

THE WATERFALL AT KLEINTOBEL
1919 · Oil · 58¹/₂ x 46³/₄ inches · Private Collection

This landscape, which at first glance looks like a chaos of violent color contrasts (red next to green, blue next to yellow), proves on closer study to be a magnificently expressed vision of the gigantic primeval presence of mountains. To left and right slopes dotted with fir trees rise toward unknown heights. Between them foams a mountain stream whose source must lie far beyond the tremendous boulders that some giant's hand seems to have hurled down into the gorge. This is nature in its first state, intensified and made articulate by color that reaches far beyond nature. The explosive handling of the paint adds to the vitality.

ERNST LUDWIG KIRCHNER · THE WATERFALL
AT KLEINTOBEL

Landscape near Caslano

Fruit and Pitcher

CARL HOFER · 1878—1955

Hofer entered the Academy of his native Karlsruhe in 1896 to study under Hans Thoma and Leopold Kalckreuth. From 1902 to 1908 he lived in Rome, from 1908 to 1913 in Paris. Under the influence of Cézanne he arrived at a style which successfully combined a classical attitude much like that of Hans von Marées (a painter to whom Hofer was very close at the beginning of his career) and an Expressionist feeling. His favorite theme was young girls: slender, delicate figures whose tranquil life is suggested by harmonious colors and forms—distant cousins of Otto Müller's gypsies. He also painted landscapes and compositions containing many figures.

Hofer's wartime experiences—he was interned in France from 1914 to 1917—and the revolutionary postwar climate dispelled the calm serenity reflected in his early work; its idyllic mood gave way to a darkly threatening, often spectral one. Forms became more angular and tense, colors more expressive; shapes were reduced to symbolic simplicity. In the mid-twenties, especially in his Ticino landscapes, his color became gentler and acquired greater richness and harmony, but this change was soon overshadowed by threatening events in the outside world. In 1933 Hofer was dismissed from his teaching position at the Berlin Academy. In 1943 much of his work was destroyed in air raids, and when World War II ended his style changed again. He turned to abstraction as a means of reflecting a chaotically turbulent world where hellishly distorted faces, weird demons and terrifying animals celebrate mad orgies, and where death, destruction and baseness hold sway.

HEAD OF A GIRL
1920 · Oil · 22¹/₄ x 19¹/₈ inches · Galerie des 20. Jahrhunderts, Berlin

A portrait sketched in Hofer's rapid, sure brushwork. Its cool tones all harmonize with blue and gray. The value contrasts lead up to a focal point in the light parts of the girl's head, which seems to shine with a light of its own beneath the tight cap of hair. All this conveys the cool reserve character of the model—or the character attributed to her by the artist.

CARL HOFER · HEAD OF A GIRL

Frau Strathmann

Pink Roses

LOVIS CORINTH · 1858—1925

Lovis Corinth, the son of a tanner and farmer, was born in Tapiau, East Prussia. Of all the German Impressionists he is the one who most deserves to be called a "painter" in the true sense. He entered the Königsberg Academy in 1876 and encountered Impressionism first in Munich in 1880 and then in Paris in 1884. From the start he was a follower of French *plein air* painting but did not utilize its insights merely to reproduce the visible world. He painted portraits, nudes, still lifes, and landscapes (the latter chiefly in his later years), as well as mythological and religious subjects, and was certainly one of the most versatile personalities among German painters of the nineteenth and early twentieth centuries.

Corinth was familiar with avant-garde art without being challenged by it. He remained committed to nature all his life, although the spiritual and intellectual bankruptcy of the years following World War I disturbed him deeply and made him wonder whether this commitment was not a mistake and whether painting's real task might not be to present the unreal. His temperament was impulsive but inhibited, with a depressive tendency. Especially toward the end of his life he gave such rein to his instinct for strong, expressive color that his landscapes, close to nature as they are, sometimes approach the passionate expressivity that characterizes the *Brücke* painters.

EASTER ON THE WALCHENSEE
1922 · Oil · 23⅝ x 31¼ inches · Private Collection

After World War I Corinth bought a small property on the banks of the Walchensee in Upper Bavaria, and the lake was the subject of many of his last pictures. This one, showing Corinth's rapidity of brush technique and sureness of color, seeks to capture the feeling of winter turning into spring: snow-covered mountains, cool blue water, trees with traces of colorful autumn foliage caught in their

branches, patches of grass where the fresh green of the new growth fights to establish itself against the withered brown. But bright as the picture is, its serene, Easterlike tranquillity is not entirely untroubled. The deep tones of blue along the banks of the lake and the gloomy, rather unfriendly violet of the hills introduce a chilly note like an echo of the painter's own depressed frame of mind.

LOVIS CORINTH · EASTER ON THE WALCHENSEE

Gypsy Girls with Sunflowers   *Gypsy in a Garden*

OTTO MÜLLER · 1874—1930

Otto Müller received his elementary training in painting at the Dresden Academy between 1895 and 1898 but after that was self-taught. In 1910 he became a member of the Dresden group of artists known as *Die Brücke* (The Bridge) and an associate of Ernst Ludwig Kirchner, Erich Heckel and Karl Schmidt-Rottluff. From the outset his theme was man as a created being, and especially the existence of inexperienced young women, who seemed to him closer than men to the organic cycles of nature. Müller's mother was a gypsy, but this alone does not explain why he made gypsy women his theme. These unsophisticated girls seemed to him the most appropriate models for the uncorrupted humanity he wanted to portray. His purpose, however, was not purely descriptive; he wanted to recapture a paradise of quiet, harmonious union between man and nature. It is easy to see why he avoided the violent, shocking stridency of color that his associates used, preferring soft, pastel-like tonalities which give all his paintings a lyrical, idyllic quality. This feeling, together with the free, close-to-nature vitality that emanates from his graceful girls, slender as reeds, with their long legs and pointed breasts, made his paintings symbols of a new Arcadia.

GYPSY WOMEN
1925 · Oil · 58¹/₂ x 38¹/₄ inches · Collection Herbert Kurz, Wolframs-Eschenbach

An alternative title for this picture might be "The Stages of Life." It shows four figures, ranging from the helpless, naked baby on the left, through the girl holding the child and the one on the threshold of aware, experienced womanhood, to the old woman dimly glimpsed through the open door as a distorted, shadowy face. Her relegation to a remote, inaccessible region is typical of Müller; his work held no place for old age and decay. What he was trying to capture, here and throughout his painting, was unreflective being, enhanced by a delicate elegiac note. The mood is echoed in the restrained colors and the apathetic unawareness of the girls.

OTTO MÜLLER · GYPSY WOMEN

Song of the Mocking Bird

Überland

PAUL KLEE · 1879—1940

Paul Klee was born in Münchenbuchsee near Bern, where his father was a music teacher. He may well be the most versatile artistic personality of this century with the exception of Picasso; certainly he is one of the most attractive. There is no trend in modern painting that is not represented in his *œuvre* of drawings and graphic art, water colors and oils. Expressionism, Cubism, Surrealism, and abstraction are all to be found, although Klee never followed any of these movements exclusively. He drew his themes from all areas of the seen and the unseen, but especially from that inexhaustible intermediate zone where the realms of mind and matter touch.

The musical talent he inherited from his father—he originally thought of becoming a musician—enriched his art. In 1898 he became a pupil of Franz Stuck at the Munich Academy, but he resisted academicism and by 1900 was producing strongly expressive prints and drawings, media which occupied him until the beginning of World War I. Soon, however, a lyrical, poetic element emerged, which became very pronounced about 1910 and was to be a permanent characteristic—a reminder of his musical heritage. This lyricism survived all the stimulating new ideas he was exposed

to in his productive friendships with Wassily Kandinsky, Franz Marc and August Macke in the *Blaue Reiter* (Blue Rider), as well as his encounter with modern French painting, and reached its full development when he discovered color for its own sake. This happened during a stay in Tunisia. Klee saw color as an essential element in his work, and he exploited its whole gamut, from utmost delicacy to full vehemence.

In 1920 Walter Gropius invited him to teach at the Bauhaus, and he remained there until 1931, when he went to the Düsseldorf Academy. Persecuted as a "degenerate artist," he left Germany for Switzerland in 1933. His last twenty years in Germany were enormously productive, and he even found time to publish some fundamental ideas on art and its aims in *Schöpferische Konfession* (1920), *On Modern Art* (1924) and *Pedagogical Sketchbook* (1925). The serenely aloof, sometimes ironical calmness of his work of the 1920's, chiefly intimate, small-format pictures with a dreamy musical quality, gave way toward the end of the decade to an equally appealing mellow, symbolic style which used larger forms and grew increasingly abstract.

THE GOLDEN FISH
1925 · Oil · 19⅜ x 27 inches · Kunsthalle Hamburg

A luminous golden body in a soundless but mysteriously animated aquarium world, the fish of the title emerges from the mystical darkness that surrounds it like a halo. This is not *a* fish but the

essence of *fish*. By means of quite realistic images (water plants, ripples, other fishes) Klee has transformed it and its existential world, so foreign yet so attractive to man, into a magical poem.

PAUL KLEE · THE GOLDEN FISH

The Bridge in the Park   *Clown*

ERICH HECKEL · 1883—1970

Heckel was born in Döbeln, Saxony, and studied architecture at the Dresden Technische Hochschule together with Karl Schmidt-Rottluff, with whom he was later to pursue common goals. In 1905 he and Ernst Ludwig Kirchner founded *Die Brücke* (The Bridge), and in 1906 Heckel decided to make painting his career. Until World War I, in which he served his full four years as an enlisted man, he painted chiefly portraits and landscapes composed of flat, angular, jagged forms and linear structures reminiscent of woodcuts. Nevertheless these early pictures have a soulful, almost lyrical tone which, as the war approached, was replaced by a threatening, inflammatory one—a premonition of things to come. The change of mood affected Heckel's palette too, but he was so averse to disharmony of any kind that before the war was over he was reverting to a romantic sensitivity, and during the 1920's this completely re-established itself.

From 1918 to 1941 Heckel lived in Berlin but traveled considerably. Landscapes became his favorite theme, treated in a tender, almost realistic style in oil, water color and graphic media. This, however, did not prevent him from being outlawed by the Nazis in 1937 as a "degenerate artist." Heckel lived in Carinthia from 1941 to 1943. In 1944, after the destruction of his home and studio in Berlin, he returned to Germany, to Hemmenhofen on Lake Constance. During these years his forms became firmer, and many of the characteristics of his *Brücke* period reappeared, with the difference that the maturity of age has obliterated all that was tentative or uncertain.

MOUNTAIN VILLAGE
1925 · Oil · 29¹/₄ x 26 inches · Private Collection

The atmosphere of a lower Alpine valley in spring is captured in a realistic style that would never identify the painting as the work of an artist who a few years previously had been using harsh, strident forms and colors. We are reminded of the German romantic landscapists' efforts to catch the charm of Alpine slopes rising steeply into the towering mountains.

ERICH HECKEL · MOUNTAIN VILLAGE

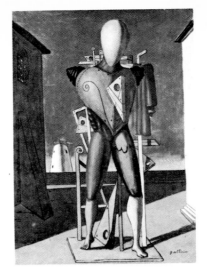

*Metaphysical Landscape
with White Tower*

Hector's Return

GIORGIO DE CHIRICO · 1888—

Giorgio de Chirico was born to Italian parents in Volvo in Greece. He spent two years at the Athens Academy, but his most important formative influence was his encounter with Italian Renaissance painting about 1905. In the museums of Milan and Florence he copied Uccello and Piero della Francesco, acquiring a feeling for big, monumental form which was reinforced by Arnold Böcklin and Max Klinger with whom he studied at the Munich Academy in 1909. In 1911 he went to Paris, joined the avant-garde and got to know Picasso, who strengthened so-called metaphysical tendencies which had begun to appear in his paintings of city scenes about 1910. After he returned to Italy in 1915 he developed *Pittura Meta-fisica,* which he considered an important original contribution to

painting. From 1915 to about 1924 was the period of the pictures in which objects were inflated to a monumental scale, as though destined for eternity, and often lifted out of their logical contexts into an existential world beyond the one known to us through our senses.

Returning to Paris in 1924, Chirico joined the Surrealists and until the early 1930's painted pictures in which unnatural or super-natural dreamlike elements are incorporated into the symbolic natural world of his earlier works. He then departed radically from this kind of painting and turned to straightforward descriptions of nature in the manner of Renoir, completely eliminating the fantastic. These nudes and still lifes show little creativity.

TWO HORSES BY THE SEA
1925—1930 · Oil · 21½ x 18 inches · Private Collection

Two symbolic rather than lifelike horses stand on the margin of an equally unreal sea. Their curved bodies, which suggest statues rather than warm-blooded creatures, are bathed in a strangely empty light, devoid of atmosphere. A ghostly silence emanates from

the forms and the neutral gray colors, filling the whole picture. Even the symbols of the past—the crumbling temple, the broken drum from a column—seem to exist in a world that will always remain timeless.

GIORGIO DE CHIRICO · TWO HORSES BY THE SEA

Homage to Oskar Panizza　　　　　*The Mechanic Hartfield*

GEORGE GROSZ · 1893—1959

George Grosz's parents wanted him to become an army officer or government official, but he was expelled from school and decided to become an artist. He was admitted to the Dresden Academy in 1909 at the age of sixteen. In 1913 he spent six months in Paris and discovered Cubism, which he rejected and parodied. In 1914 he was drafted into the army and was later wounded in action. In 1918 he joined the Berlin Dada group. From then until his departure for the United States in 1933 he pitilessly unmasked the effete bourgeoisie, the *nouveaux riches,* feudal powers, and Prussian militarism, through the medium of satirical drawings and paintings, bordering on caricature. These exposures of a rotten and hypocritical society were enlivened with a dash of Surrealism and executed in a painfully exaggerated realistic technique. They repeatedly got Grosz into trouble with the authorities. His drawings are better than his paintings, although during the 1920's he did some excellent portraits in which the satirical element is considerably subdued. After he emigrated to America in 1933, the biting irony and aggressiveness began to disappear from his other work too, from his landscapes and figurative and fantastic sketches, but he did not become bourgeois. Until his death in Berlin in 1959 Grosz never received the recognition his achievement merited. Today he has a devoted following of admirers.

THE PILLARS OF SOCIETY
1926 · Oil · Nationalgalerie, Berlin

The caustic irony and stinging sarcasm of this picture explain why Grosz never had any real friends in the German circles that might have furnished patrons for his art. Never has the mask been so mercilessly ripped from smug middle-class faces. Never have the narrow-mindedness and hypocrisy of a so-called elite, which thinks itself far above the common herd, been so pilloried. A former member of a student corps clutches his beer stein and saber as if they were attributes of student prestige. Bearing in his open cranium memories of bygone days as a proud Uhlan, which have left their stamp in his brusque demeanor, he assumes a martial stance. The bureaucrat holding a palm branch in his hand derives his great fund of wisdom from the daily papers. His head is full of thoughts of a kind plainly suggested by his unambiguous headdress. An overfed "democrat" patriotically holds up the German flag. To him Socialism is just another word for labor—other people's labor of course. The judge wears a face of hideous hypocrisy. Members of the armed services in full regalia, brandishing their arms, form a macabre background for this social pyramid.

GEORGE GROSZ · THE PILLARS OF SOCIETY

Lotte Franzos   *Lübeck: The Jakobskirche*

OSKAR KOKOSCHKA · 1886—

Oskar Kokoschka was born in Austria, at Pöchlarn on the Danube. The African and South Pacific art he saw in museums while he was still a child made an impression that partly determined the direction his artistic talent would take. He entered the Vienna Kunstgewerbeschule in 1904 and it became his home until 1908. He produced his first oil paintings in 1907 at the age of twenty at the same time as his earliest dramatic works, *Hoffnung der Frauen* and *Sphinx und Strohmann*. The latter were not without influence on literary Expressionism, and Kokoschka continued to write plays for many years. At first he had no success as a painter. The colored lithographs he exhibited in 1908 as illustrations for his own book *Die Träumenden Knaben* aroused such an outcry that the young artist was forced to leave the Kunstgewerbeschule. The eminent architect Adolf Loos offered him support and encouragement at this time.

Between 1908 and 1913 Kokoschka painted many portraits which rank among his best works. They show a penetrating insight into his subject that approaches depth psychology and reveal an agonizing need for self-expression. He went at the character of the poets, actors and distinguished intellectuals he painted through a translucent color and labyrinthine design whose sole purpose seems in the end to have been to expose the subject's nervous system. Landscapes were treated in the same probing psychological fashion.

Immediately before World War I Kokoschka's painting reached an explosive pitch. Dispensing with a brush, he would fling paint at the canvas with his hand or a palette knife in veritable orgies of color. From 1915 to 1916 he served at the front and was severely wounded. After being discharged, he at first spent most of his time writing, but returned to painting when he was appointed to the faculty of the Dresden Academy in 1919. This period was one of Biblical themes, landscapes and city scenes; it reached its climax in the numerous urban landscapes he painted during his travels in 1924.

Political unrest in Austria after the murder of Dollfuss in 1934 caused Kokoschka to flee to Prague. After the Munich agreement of 1938 he escaped to London, his work having meantime been proscribed as "degenerate" in Germany. His war years in England produced pictures of deep emotion and a sense of human degradation. In 1955 he went to live in Villeneuve on Lake Geneva. He remains one of the significant artists of the twentieth century.

LYONS
1927 · Oil · 37⅞ x 50¾ inches · The Phillips Collection, Washington, D. C.

The individual character of the French city of Lyons is captured in Kokoschka's translucent color and in the vibrant agitation of his drawing and form. Here, as in all his city pictures, what he was aiming at was not a painted photograph; he was trying to convey the specific atmosphere of Lyons. The viewer is drawn into the picture as if he were hovering with the seagulls above the landscape.

OSKAR KOKOSCHKA · LYONS

Left Profile   *Group of Four*

OSKAR SCHLEMMER · 1888—1943

Oskar Schlemmer, who was born in Stuttgart, studied under Hölzel at the Stuttgart Academy in the years before World War I. He took form rather than color for his domain, concentrating almost exclusively on integrating the form of the human body into the picture space. His concept was by no means naturalistic; especially in his murals and stage sets he created monumental scenes of life and action which have an archaic austerity and rank among the most beautiful and original works of German modernism.

FOUR HEADS
1928 · Oil · 17¹/₈ x 12¹/₂ inches · Private Collection

In the right half of the picture four impersonal, dramatically elongated heads, simplified into symbols, move into position one behind the other; the rounded curve of the shoulders becomes part of the movement. The progression from back view to full profile epitomizes the human head moving in space—a space created by the contrast between the colorless left half of the picture and the sequence of head shapes on the right, as well as by the almost atmospheric lightening of colors from foreground to background.

OSKAR SCHLEMMER · FOUR HEADS

Wendelsweg in Frankfurt am Main   *Self-Portrait with Statue*

MAX BECKMANN · 1884—1950

Beckmann, a native of Leipzig, studied from 1899 to 1903 at the Weimar Academy. He came to know Impressionism, which dominated his work until World War I, in Florence and Paris and in Berlin, where he lived from 1909 to 1914. He served briefly in the German Army, then in 1915 went to live in Frankfurt am Main. In 1925 he became a professor at the school of art there, but was dismissed in 1933 by the Nazi regime. His wartime experiences, postwar social and moral decadence and the political unrest and excesses of this turbulent period affected him profoundly and led him to his major theme: man threatened by a chaotic, disrupted world. Even before the end of World War I he began to portray man in a way that constituted an indictment of the general bankruptcy, giving him an ugly, uncouth aspect. The individual was shown relegated to hopelessly lonely exile; as a member of a group he was seen imprisoned in a threatening, caste-ridden world with no exit, at the mercy of a reality more animal than human. Beckmann was very close to Otto Dix and George Grosz, although he never went in for their biting social criticism. He himself said that his personal, expressive style of painting was intended to reflect his sense of life.

From 1933 to 1937 Beckmann lived in Berlin. He then went to Paris and later to Amsterdam where he stayed until 1947. In the 1930's began the gradual transition, marked by the first of his great triptychs, toward his more monumental period of maturity and old age, when he turned away from the trivialities of daily life in favor of mythological subjects. But to the last his central theme remained the reality of man. The knowledge of it that he had gained from personal experience, never serene but always bearing the scars of inward suffering and isolation, left its clear imprint on his work.

Beckmann died in the United States in 1950.

RUGBY PLAYERS
1921 · Oil · Städtisches Kunstmuseum, Duisburg

The piled-up forms, the cool colors and the crisscross design containing the action in a kind of latticework are all characteristic of Beckmann's work after the mid-1920's. This picture shows not a specific episode in the game but the game itself, the passionate struggle for victory. The players overreach one another like a pyramid of bodies whose apex is the ball; the striped goalpost boldly states itself as the center of action. There is nothing serene about this picture, which captures the fanaticism of the struggle for the ball and the utter exhaustion of a fight that knows no quarter. (See the player at the base of the goalpost.) One player has been brought to his knees in a tackle; another is being ruthlessly shoved aside by the man holding the ball. But the shout of "Goal!" that will release the tension does not come. The interaction of subject and technique is extraordinary.

MAX BECKMANN · RUGBY PLAYERS

House on Pamet River
1934 · Water color · 19³/₄ x 24⁷/₈ inches · Whitney Museum of American Art,
New York

Second-Story Sunlight
1960 · Oil on canvas · 40 x 50 inches · Whitney Museum of American Art,
New York (Gift of the Friends of the Whitney Museum of
American Art, and purchase)

EDWARD HOPPER · 1882—1967

Edward Hopper was born in Nyack, New York, in 1882. He studied at the school run by William M. Chase in New York, but a greater influence was the instruction he received from Robert Henri. His early painting was done in a dark manner, but his palette brightened after a stay in Paris (1906—1907). Though his etchings won him early recognition, he was less successful with his paintings. An oil "Sailing," exhibited at the 1913 Armory Show, sold promptly, but it was a full decade before his next sale, when the Brooklyn Museum showed his water colors. It was only then that he could give up his work as an illustrator, through which he had supported himself and his wife for many years, and devote himself exclusively to his painting. While he won many awards and had numerous exhibitions in leading museums, his private life remained quiet and reserved.

After a brief period of experimental painting while in Paris, he concentrated on creating an art of intense realism from the materials of the familiar world. He once defined his credo: "Instead of subjectivity, a new objectivity; instead of abstraction, a reaffirmation of representation and specific subject matter; instead of internationalism, an art based on the American scene."

Hopper's interest vacillated between New England and New York. Yet, in all of his paintings, architecture plays a leading role.

Often the houses and streets seem uninhabited, and a sense of drama is created by the very absence of people. But even where human figures appear, they are not really people, but simply types. But whether people are absent or not, a feeling of isolation and loneliness is always present. One is often reminded of Maurice Utrillo's early paintings of Montmartre.

Hopper's matter-of-fact quality is also reminiscent of Winslow Homer and Thomas Eakins. He set his goals modestly but firmly: "My aim in painting has always been the most exact transcription possible of my most intimate impressions of nature." He also said that all he wanted to do was to "paint sunlight on the side of a house." There can be no doubt that his essential subject is light which defines mood and scene. Fascinated by everyday sights rather than by splendor, he presents the world he knows—a small-town street, a Victorial mansion, a cafeteria, a movie theater—always in the sharp, glaring light. His effort was toward simplification, toward the omission of naturalistic detail. He created archetypes of American life with an austere poetry that has found many admirers. As Sam Hunter wrote: "Without the precedent of Hopper, it would be difficult to conceive such varied and distinct poetic documentation of the American scene of the late thirties and early forties as those of Ben Shahn, Walter Stuempfig and Loren MacIver."

EARLY SUNDAY MORNING
1930 · Oil on canvas · 35 x 60 inches · Whitney Museum of American Art, New York

Simple buildings like this one can be found in every small American town. Yet few men have the eyes to perceive the strange beauty of its horizontals and verticals, its red, brown and black rectangles,

enlivened by the verticals of a hydrant and barberpole. Out of a drab subject Hopper created a fine picture that captures a mood of sober melancholy.

EDWARD HOPPER · EARLY SUNDAY MORNING

Girl with Black Hair

Bright Mountain and Valley

ALEXEI VON JAWLENSKY · 1864—1941

Alexei von Jawlensky was born in Kuslovo in Russia. He had been intended for an army career but in 1889 he discovered a bent for painting and took some courses at the St. Petersburg Academy. In 1896 he resigned his captain's commission and left for Munich with Marianne von Werefkin. His contact with Wassily Kandinsky, with his fellow-members of the *Neue Künstlervereinigung* (New Artists' Association) and with the *Blaue Reiter* (Blue Rider) painters reinforced his conviction that his future lay in painting. Nevertheless he went his own way, which was that of the Fauves rather than Kandinsky or the *Blaue Reiter*. His themes were limited to still lifes and human figures, especially heads, painted in strong, clear forms and forceful, glowing colors which soon acquired the richness of stained glass windows in sunlight. His style was never imitative. Although he stayed close to the motif at first—some of his heads are almost portraits—his touch infused everything with the unreality of a still life. This tendency increased noticeably after World War I. His heads began to take on a spiritual expression; his heart-felt artistic sensitivity gave them the transcendental quality of Russian icons. The same inwardness marks his last pictures, which are simplified down to symbols.

ROSES IN A BLUE VASE WITH FIGURINE
OF A FLUTEPLAYER
1931 · Oil · 19¹/₂ x 8¹/₂ inches · Private Collection

The extraordinary intensity Jawlensky could give his colors is well illustrated by the red background, the green apple and the somewhat more restrained blue of the slim, tubular vase. Yet there is nothing aggressive about the picture. Its tone is set by the harmonious colors. The little fluteplayer figurine introduces an idyllic note and its colors blend discreetly into the foreground.

158

ALEXEI VON JAWLENSKY · ROSES IN A BLUE VASE
WITH FIGURINE OF A FLUTEPLAYER

The Subway
1928 · Oil on canvas · 16¹/₈ x 22¹/₈ inches
The Museum of Modern Art, New York
(Gift of Abby Aldrich Rockefeller)

Zapatistas
1913 · Oil on canvas · 55 x 45 inches
The Museum of Modern Art, New York

JOSÉ CLEMENTE OROZCO · 1883—1949

Orozco, born in a small town in the state of Jalisco, Mexico, moved to Mexico City when still a child. He attended night courses in drawing at the Academy of Fine Art of San Carlos, but then against his wishes, spent three years at a school of agriculture. He next studied architecture, only to return to art and to the Academy, where Diego Rivera was a fellow-student. Unlike Rivera, Orozco played no part in the national revolution of 1910, except for contributing satirical drawings to a revolutionary magazine. Dissatisfied with conditions in Mexico, torn between revolution and counterrevolution, he spent part of 1917 in San Francisco and New York.

Though he had already painted genre scenes with unsentimental forcefulness and pictures with Mexican revolutionary content, his great period began in 1922, with the birth of large-scale mural painting in Mexico. In color that was at first subdued and later became very strong, he painted frescoes in the National Preparatory School, the House of Tiles and the Industrial School at Orizaba. His style grew monumental and expressionist. From 1927 until 1930 he was again in the United States, where he was commissioned to decorate the walls of the refectory at Pomona College in California and a large hall of the New School for Social Research, New York City. After a trip to Europe in 1932, he returned to the United

States and painted murals for the library of Dartmouth College.

From 1934 until his death fifteen years later, he executed many large murals, the most outstanding being those for the Palace of Fine Arts in Mexico City and the University and Orphanage in Guadalajara. Shortly before his death he completed a mural in the National Historical Museum at Chapultepec Castle, Mexico City, on the theme of the national leader Juarez and the reforms he inaugurated. Orozco's death in 1949 was mourned by all of Mexico.

Though Orozco did many excellent drawings and oils, his most important works are his dramatic murals. In them he often dealt with Mexican folk mythology and national history, as well as religion. Though he belonged to no political party (unlike the other two giants of Mexican art, Rivera and Siqueiros, who joined the Communist party) his own art is political propaganda in the noblest sense. His frescoes cry out against machine-age values, against the abuses of capitalism and the carnage of warfare. A Guatemalan poet, Luis Cardoza y Aragon, who was closely associated with him, wrote: "He has never cultivated appearance, falsely interpreted a single voice, or eluded dangers. He has shown no weaknesses nor has he made concessions to spurious tastes, to present exigencies. His art possesses the dignity of this life; it is built not on motives of today, but on those of eternity."

THE BARRICADE
1931 · Oil on canvas · 55 x 45 inches · The Museum of Modern Art, New York

At the height of his career and international fame, the artist recalled a past, when brawny, armed peasants gathered to fight the forces of reaction. Though not an active participant in the social and political struggle that started about 1910, Orozco frequently depicted those Mexican peasant groups who roamed the country

and risked their lives in the war for a just reform of the obsolete land laws, for a better social order. A slightly different version of this picture can be found in the fresco Orozco made for the National Preparatory School in Mexico. It provides an idea of the monumentality of his vision.

160

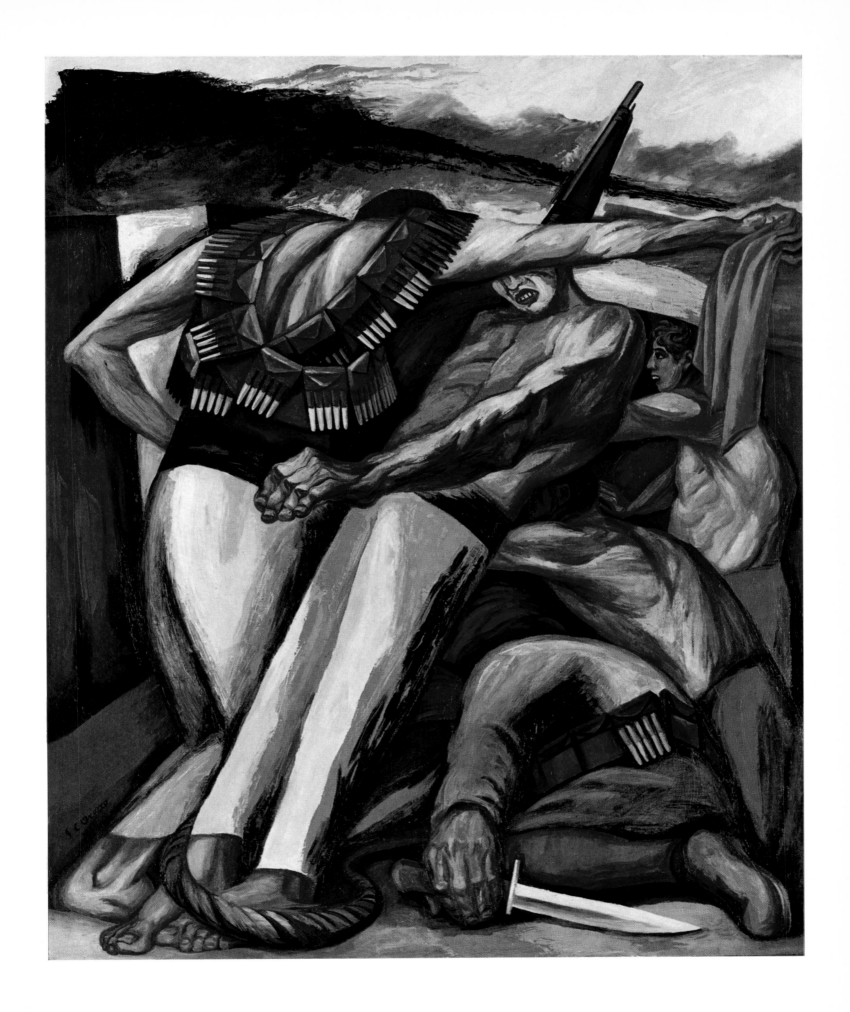

JOSÉ CLEMENTE OROZCO · THE BARRICADE

Anemones   *Still Life*

GEORGES BRAQUE · 1882—1963

Georges Braque, the son of a housepainter, was born in Argenteuil, grew up in Le Havre, and in 1900 went to live in Paris, where he spent the rest of his life except for brief wartime absences. He began as a Fauve, but about 1906 adopted a more architectural style using more restrained colors whose purpose was almost the opposite of that of the Fauves. Under the influence of Cézanne and of his friend Picasso, Braque developed an even greater liking for structured composition, thereby leading to the geometrical stylization that between 1908 and 1910 gave birth to Cubism. Convinced that in painting, which is in the last analysis an arrangement of planes, every nuance of representational color can be assigned to its own specific plane, and that the object can be made to emerge in its essential form by constructing such planes, he arrived at analytical Cubism at the same time as Picasso, who had approached it from different directions. Working together, Braque and Picsaso systematically developed it into a soundly based system which could be applied to the human form, still lifes and landscapes.

About 1912 a shift from analysis to synthesis became noticeable in Braque and other Cubists. The formal elements arrived at by analysis were utilized to build up objects, not break them down. But World War I prevented Braque from pursuing this process to its logical conclusion, as it also stopped him from developing his newly discovered technique of *papiers collés,* in which printed letters of the alphabet were incorporated into the painting, sand was mixed with the paint, and fragments of all kinds of material were glued to the canvas.

By the time he was discharged from the army in 1917 Cubism had changed, as individual painters developed it in different directions, and Braque turned away from it, although he never relinquished it altogether. Until the early 1930's his nudes, still lifes and compositions with figures were again more closely related to reality, and his earlier abstract tendency grew less pronounced. About 1930 he shifted to a non-representational type of painting, monumental in its simplicity of color and form, in which quite undistinguished things such as a body of water or a bowl became the subject of a telling painting. However far Braque departed from the visible he never rejected it completely. All his work, including his sculpture, reflects his steadfast love of physical things, even the most commonplace ones.

WOMAN WITH A MANDOLIN

1937 · Oil · 51¼ x 38¼ inches · The Museum of Modern Art, New York (Mrs. Simon Guggenheim Fund)

This work dates from the period that began about 1930 when Braque reverted to a more abstract, constructive treatment of the motif. The intimate relationship with material reality that had characterized the two preceding decades was replaced by architectural discipline and a two-dimensional technique. The picture centers on the blue-black figure of the woman, reduced to painterly symbolism. Within the outlines of the figure explanatory lines have been scratched in with the brush handle. Around the woman the intimate world of the music room has been compiled item by item: the music stand, the vaselike table lamp, the papered wall, and all the other things that make up the still ambience of the statuesque mandolin player.

162

GEORGES BRAQUE · WOMAN WITH A MANDOLIN

Dancers

Oriental Poppies

EMIL NOLDE · 1867—1956

Emil Hansen, a farmer's son born in 1867 in the village of Nolde in northern Schleswig, adopted the name of his birthplace in 1901. His inclination for the visual arts showed itself in early childhood, but in 1884 he was apprenticed to a furniture manufacturer in Flensburg to learn ornamental wood carving. By 1888 he was earning his living at this and drawing and painting and taking courses at the Karlsruhe Kunstgewerbeschule in his free time. In 1889 he moved to Berlin; in 1892 he became a teacher of ornamental drawing and modeling at the museum of industrial arts in St. Gallen, where he spent seven years. Here he began to draw landscapes and heads and to paint in water color, still as a hobby. However, some postcard reproductions of "mountain scenes" proved so successful that in 1898 he decided to devote himself entirely to painting.

Nolde began in a Impressionist style, but the influence of his fellow-painters in *Die Brücke* (The Bridge), to which he belonged for a short time between 1906 and 1907, and of Edvard Munch, Van Gogh and James Ensor led him about 1905 to Expressionism. This movement set the course of all his later work and he became one of its great masters. The descriptive landscapes he had been painting gave way to figure paintings, and his urge to depict elemental visionary experiences found its outlet principally in religious themes. In both oil paintings and water colors Nolde's primary medium was always full-blooded, sensuous, symbolic color. His innate feeling for the natural and the elemental and for the mystical forces of life and nature gave his style a forceful expressiveness, no matter what the motif might be—landscape, flowers or people. He traveled extensively but in 1927 retired to Seebüll in Schleswig, a rural spot which satisfied his love of nature and was his home until his death.

FRISIAN FARMSTEAD ON A CANAL
1935 · Oil · 28¹/₂ x 34³/₈ inches · Private Collection

"In the face of nature, full, saturated colors have been my best friends." The strong tones of this Frisian landscape bear out Nolde's words, as do all his other descriptions of nature. Under a heavy evening sky in which two fluffy clouds seem to float in a boundless sea, the narrow strip of dark green plain and the blue wedge of canal and bridge reach yearningly into an empty distance. Beside the dark form of the farmhouse, the autumnal gold of a haystack stands out in the twilight as if caught in the last rays of the setting sun. Nolde has captured the mood of a fall day drawing to its close over the plain of his native northern Germany as perfectly as he has conveyed the essence of a landscape losing itself in infinite space. It hardly occurs to us that the color is exaggerated or that the picture is not a rendering of a specific scene but an imaginative statement by the painter about the landscape.

EMIL NOLDE · FRISIAN FARMSTEAD ON A CANAL

Hindu Woman

Homage to Bach

RAOUL DUFY · 1877—1953

In 1892, after working for a time for a firm of coffee importers, Dufy entered the École des Beaux-Arts in Le Havre, the town where he was born. There he met Othon Friesz, whom he followed to the studio of Léon Bonnat in Paris in 1900. As he got to know the works of Van Gogh, Gauguin, Monet and Pissarro, the academic style in which he had been working (chiefly in water color) was superseded by an Impressionist one, and later, about 1905, by a Fauve period strongly influenced by Matisse. Then he discovered and explored Cézanne and Cubism. Painting, however, brought him little material reward and in 1912 he readily accepted an offer from the couturier Paul Poiret to design dress and furnishing fabrics, a field which offered full scope to his real gift, a remarkable decorative sense. This in turn affected his painting, and in the

1920's he achieved his own style. The firm Cubistic color planes began to merge. His landscapes, still lifes and portraits acquired a childish, story-book atmosphere, created by strong but delicately harmonized colors, swiftly and freely applied. These works show Dufy to have been one of the greatest painter-poets in modern art.

Dufy traveled extensively. His most important work, artistically as well as in size—it is over six thousand square feet in area—was the mural entitled "Electricity" he did for the Paris Exhibition of 1937. Besides painting, he continued to design fabrics, experimented with ceramics and did stage design and book illustrations. Like Renoir, he suffered from arthritis which made his work increasingly difficult and finally impossible. He was successfully treated in 1950, but he died three years later.

THE CORONATION OF GEORGE VI
1937 · 8¹/₄ x 10 inches · Collection M. Baulard

Dufy has recorded the coronation of the King of England in a sort of documentary snapshot executed in his characteristic later manner: in quick shorthand outlines and bright, transparent colors. But the color is not carefully or naturalistically confined within the

outlines of the objects in the picture. This is obvious in the pale violet oval area which surrounds the royal coach like a halo and almost imperceptibly yet tellingly singles out this part of the picture as the focus of attention.

RAOUL DUFY · THE CORONATION OF GEORGE VI

"Wall Painting" in Black and Pink

Faust Shadow I

WILLI BAUMEISTER · 1889—1955

Willi Baumeister, who was born and died in Stuttgart, was a loner all his life. He was open to what was going on in art elsewhere but his Swabian temperament may have prevented him from joining groups such as the *Brücke* or the *Blaue Reiter*. He began as a decorator and from 1906 to 1910 he studied under Adolf Hoelzel at the Stuttgart Academy. Being more interested in form than expression, he was drawn to what the followers of Cézanne were doing in France and during two visits to Paris in 1912 and 1914 he thoroughly explored Cézanne's work. His contact with Fernand Léger was also an important stimulus in the evolution of his own style.

Baumeister achieved his first notable success with the "wall paintings" he did about 1920, which are not paintings so much as works of mural art executed in paint mixed with sand in a sort of relief technique. His efforts to give the picture surface a plastic texture by means of sand or strips of wood make him one of the forerunners of Tactilism. In the later 1920's he produced several series of paintings dealing with sport and machinery in which his sense for constructive composition proved itself. In 1936 he turned to completely abstract painting, often with Surrealist overtones, striving urgently toward primal form. The Eidos pictures, one of which is illustrated, are typical exemples of this phase. During World War II he became interested in primitive cultures: cave paintings, prehistoric sculpture and ancient Indian art, and this inspired a great many of the paintings he produced in an explosive outburst of productivity in the postwar years. Big monumental pictures, as abstract and resonant as their titles—"Montaru," "Bluxao," "Kussaua," for example—round out Baumeister's *œuvre*.

EIDOS V

1939 · Oil · 39¹/₈ x 31³/₄ inches · Bavarian State Collections, Munich

In a desert "landscape," amoebalike color forms intertwine in the company of other forms having the transparency of water. We feel as if we were face to face with formless matter striving to take shape on the day before the creation of the world.

WILLI BAUMEISTER · EIDOS V

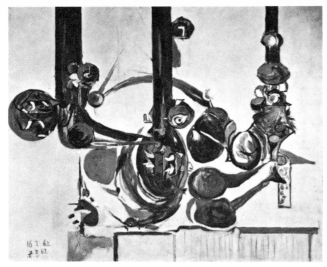

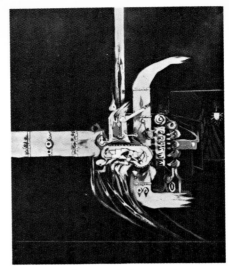

Three Suspended Forms

Machine on Black Ground

GRAHAM SUTHERLAND · 1903—

Graham Sutherland, a Londoner, began as a book illustrator and etcher. Until about 1930 he was very much under the influence of William Blake and he did not achieve his own characteristic style until after World War II. Before this he painted chiefly landscapes recalling the early improvisations of Wassily Kandinsky. After about 1945 he pursued a strangely morbid, Surrealistic realism in which the visible is transformed into a "reality" of tortured, thorny forms painted in deep, austere tones. No doubt his war experiences were partly responsible for this idiom, which seems designed to describe mankind and nature in torment. It even leaves its unmistakable stamp upon the genre in which, despite widespread criticism, Southerland has achieved great popularity: the portrait.

MEADOW PATH
1939 · Oil · 23³/₈ x 19¹/₂ inches · Tate Gallery, London

Although the picture certainly does not describe in any representational way what we see and feel on a walk across the meadows, such a stroll is clearly echoed in the blue-shadowed leaves and the differentiated greens. Knowing that this painting was preceded by studies from nature, we can see that the composition as a whole is dictated exclusively by an artistic principle: rhythmic organization of the picture-space and orchestration of the carefully harmonized colors to achieve a concerted overall effect.

GRAHAM SUTHERLAND · MEADOW PATH

Head of a Woman

Fruit

PIERRE BONNARD · 1867—1947

Pierre Bonnard was born in Fontenay-aux-Roses near Paris. He received a thorough humanistic education and at his father's insistence began in 1885 to study law. Three years later, however, he enrolled in the École des Beaux-Arts, where he met his future associates Édouard Vuillard, Maurice Denis and Paul Sérusier. He and his friends were so enthusiastic over an exhibition of Gauguin's works that they founded the group known as the Nabis who wanted to break away from Impressionism and pursue an antitheoretical kind of art that would concentrate on decorative values.

In 1889 Bonnard gave up the study of law and began his long, relatively untroubled career as a painter in which he forged steadily ahead. At first drawing and lithography were his field, and here he demonstrated an illustrative talent to which he always remained faithful, though even in his drawings he was basically a painter. In painting his theme range was to be extremely wide: landscape, nudes, portraits, interiors, still lifes, scenic motifs, and purely decorative pictures. The influence of Gauguin and, above all, of Japanese prints led him from the start to paint in flat surfaces and two-dimensional compositions of colors and lines. Color was the essential element and in fact became so much more important to him than drawing that in 1912 he himself admitted to having been so carried away by color that he had unconsciously sacrificed form. "I must practice drawing," he concluded. "I draw all the time now. After drawing will come composition, which must be balanced. A well composed picture is already half finished." About this time the peculiar "woolliness" and instability of his pictures began to tighten up and his forms became firmer. His color, however, showed a contrary tendency, taking on an Impressionist lightness and atmospheric transparency it had never had before. Both color and form retained their decorative qualities.

Although Bonnard's palette certainly became more brilliant in the last twenty-five years of his life as a result of his passion for what he called "infatuating color," it never approached the trumpet tones of the Fauves or the stridency of the Expressionists but always kept to the serene, lyrical, sunny values that make the work of this painter so appealing.

STILL LIFE WITH FRUIT

1946 · Oil · 22⁷/₈ x 13⁵/₈ inches · Galerie Maeght, Paris

This is Bonnard's last painting. It shows his infatuation with color, and proves that on the eve of his ninth decade his painting had lost none of its youthful freshness. His many canvases have won a special place in the hearts of all who love art for its joyous qualities.

PIERRE BONNARD · STILL LIFE WITH FRUIT

Landscape near Cassis

Flowers

HANS PURRMANN · 1880—1966

Hans Purrman was born in Speyer. In 1898 he began to study art at the Karlsruhe Kunstgewerbeschule after serving an apprenticeship as an ornamental painter. From 1900 to 1905 he attended the Munich Academy and in 1906 went to Paris to study with Matisse, remaining there until war broke out in 1914. Fauvism had some influence on him, but he adopted only its brilliant colors, not its two-dimensional style and use of line. Purrmann's painting kept to the old representational tradition without ever falling into shallow eclecticism. It is modern in color taste, although anything revolutionary is foreign to it: Expressionism's stridency, Cubism's rationality or Surrealism's unreality. It is modern too in its rejection of exact perspective and its non-representational color.

VIEW OVER LAKE LUGANO NEAR AGNO
1949 · Oil on canvas · Private Collection

Looking at this serene, light-drenched world, we could easily forget that it owes little to natural atmospheric effects and is constructed in a flattened manner. Two of its characteristics are the mellow, harmonious colors reminiscent of Renoir and the typical short brushstrokes with which Purrmann represented from. The viewer forgets the technical means in his joy at the scene.

HANS PURRMANN · VIEW OVER LAKE LUGANO

NEAR AGNO

Sun on the Fjord *Ox*

ROLF NESCH · 1893—

Rolf Nesch, who was born in Oberesslingen near Stuttgart, lived in Norway after 1933. He served an apprenticeship in decorative painting and in 1912 went to Dresden as a journeyman painter. Here he got to know the work of the *Brücke* (Bridge) artists, who had a formative influence on him, especially Ernst Ludwig Kirchner. He served in World War I and was a prisoner-of-war until 1919. In 1924, after several restless years of artistic groping, he went to see Kirchner—a move that was to prove decisive because that great graphic artist passed on to him almost twenty years of experience in printmaking.

Until 1925 Nesch concentrated on etching, working at first in line and outline but going on to tonal effects. Then he stumbled quite by accident on a new technique which he proceeded to develop to the full. By mistake he etched some areas on a plate too deeply so that little holes were eaten in the metal. These showed up on the print as white marks, and where the paper had been in contact with the holes it looked as if it had been embossed or stamped. Step by step Nesch developed this chance discovery into a technique of metal printing, that is to say, printing from plates which had been bent and perforated and to which a relief of wires, perforated pieces of metal and wire mesh had been soldered. About 1935 the plates themselves became relieflike, assuming the character of autonomous works of art, independent of their function in printing. From then on Nesch created almost exclusively in these two media, the print and the plate, except for some excursions into sculpture. He was always committed to outward reality—though he simplified it in a primitive way that brought it close to pure abstraction, in the 1950's even introducing Surrealist elements. This unique form of modern "painting" bordering on sculpture has an extraordinary charm.

PAN
1949 · Print · 23⅝ x 14⅜ inches · Kunsthalle, Bremen

Like man of Nesch's prints, this exists in only one copy. The head of Pan, with its big eyes and wreath of leaves and flowers, was printed from an etched zinc plate to which pieces of copper and zinc and scraps of wire mesh had been soldered. The white highlights were produced by perforations in the plate, the gray tones of the face by etching.

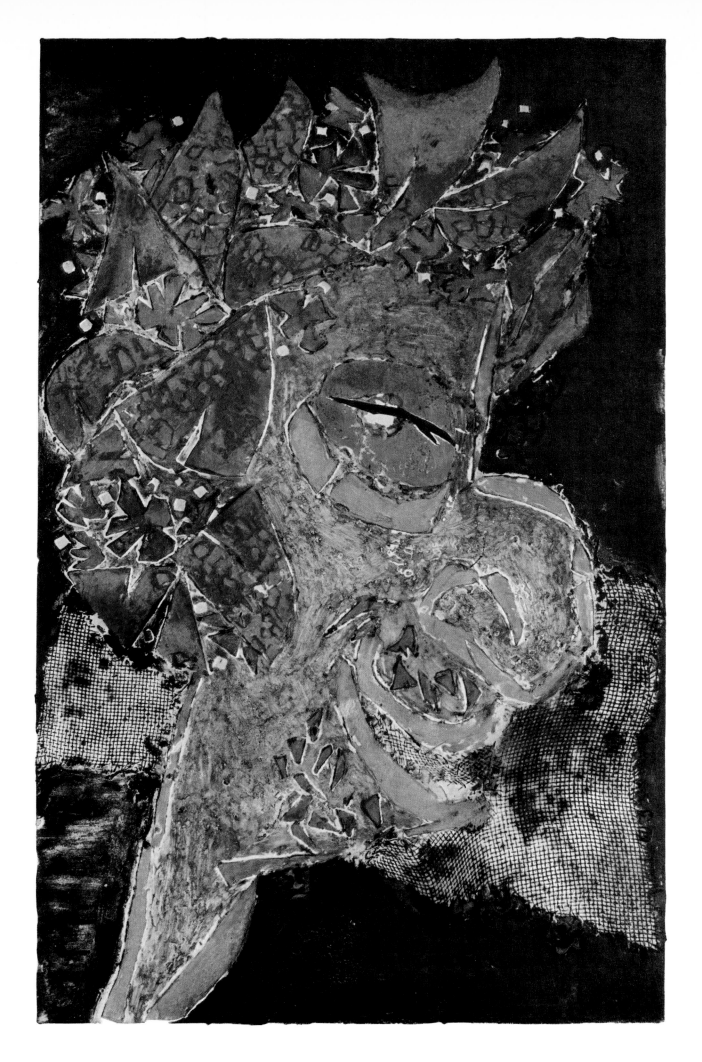

ROLF NESCH · PAN

Grand Finale

Black Paths

FRITZ WINTER · 1905—

Fritz Winter, a former miner from Altenbögge in Westphalia, came to painting by way of the Dresden Bauhaus. At first he was very close to Wassily Kandinsky and Paul Klee, but he soon developed a personal style, breaking all representational ties to nature without losing touch with it. He never looked to nature for models either in form or color, but came to regard it more and more as an arsenal of creative forces. This is especially true of his works of the time of World War II, which are particularly revealing, though limited in number. It was for good reason that Winter named a series of oil paintings done in 1944 "Motive Forces in Nature," for this title is almost a progammatic statement of his aims, at any rate until the early 1950's. He wanted to depict the life- and form-determining forces at work behind and within the seen world, and he represented them symbolically through images—images symbolizing crystal, forests, night, or the forces of growth engaged in some creative activity. Often the images are so telling that nature makes its way back into the picture not as an imitation but as a product of artistic intuition and an inward vision.

Winter's experiences as a prisoner-of-war gave the work he did about 1950 a gloomy, depressing note. After a visit to Paris in 1951 the mood became less tense and the colors more cheerful, but the curving lines that weave across the canvas (generally black and boldly painted) seem to have a function besides their compositional one: to enclose within a protective screen a world of colors which looks frail and delicate by contrast. Later his color became more prominent and succeeded in permeating the confining screen, introducing an almost romantic harmony quite in keeping with Winter's temperament.

COMPOSITION NUMBER FIVE
1949 · Oil · 37 x 43 inches · Private Collection

We look in vain for natural forms to give us a hint of what is going on, yet we cannot escape the feeling that the meeting, interpenetrating, overlapping shapes in this picture are striving to evolve. The discs seem to be centers from which tapering cellular structures floating around in an aquariumlike space derive their animation and their urge for evolution.

FRITZ WINTER · COMPOSITION NUMBER FIVE

Painting
Solomon R. Guggenheim Museum,
New York

Painting on Paper

JOAN MIRÓ · 1893—

Miró, the fourth of the great Spaniards in modern painting (the others are Picasso, Juan Gris and Salvador Dali) was born in Montroig near Barcelona. He began to study art at the Barcelona Academy when he was only fourteen. About 1912 he received great encouragement from the architect Gali who taught him the technique of terracotta painting that he has continued to use successfull. The paintings in his first exhibition (1918) showed the influence of the Fauves and Van Gogh, but in the early 1920's, after his first visit to Paris (1919) and a brief Cubist period, his future Surrealist tendency alread began to emerge. In "Farmhouse," a picture on which he worked for nine months in 1922, details remote from any logical context swarm across the canvas like scattered letters of a printed text, in the spirit of magical realism that characterized this period. Miró now pursued this direction purposefully. Never unmindful of his functions as painter, composer and colorist, as some of the Surrealists were, he invented an imaginary world where, as in some distant cosmos, semi-abstract yet not quite unnatural things and creatures lead a life of their own beyond the reaches of worldly experience. If any explicable relationship exists between them it is only because of their accidental proximity, and one suspects that they are often just meant to tease the viewer. Miró has also done stage and tapestry designs, as well as sculpture. In 1940 he left Paris because of the war and returned to his native Montroig.

WOMEN AND BIRD BY MOONLIGHT

1949 · Oil on canvas · 31⅝ x 25⅜ inches · Tate Gallery, London

If the title prompts us to look for the women, the bird and the moonlight, all we find is two hieroglyphic "woman-figures," a winged creature bearing some remote resemblance to a bird, a five-pointed star, and an unreal blue moon. Other than that, all is perplexity and unrewarding speculation. Yet however far the picture may be from reality as we know it, it conveys an impression of nocturnal happening, and this much more than the factual title is its real theme. It owes its charm, which is slightly reminiscent of the much more light-hearted works of Paul Klee, less to the few associative clues it provides than to the harmony of its colors, their interplay within a fairly confined range, and the skillful placement of the "lights" which punctuate the darkness of the night.

JOAN MIRÓ · WOMEN AND BIRD BY MOONLIGHT

Sunset
1914 · Watercolor · 16¹/₂ x 19¹/₄ inches ·
Collection, Whitney Museum
of American Art, New York

Region of Brooklyn Bridge Fantasy
1932 · Watercolor · 18³/₄ x 22¹/₄ inches ·
Collection, Whitney Museum
of American Art, New York

JOHN MARIN · 1870—1953

John Marin was born in 1870 in Rutherford, New Jersey. After studying engineering at the Stevens Institute of Technology, Hoboken, New Jersey, he worked as a draftsman in an architect's office. He was nearly thirty when he began to study painting at the Pennsylvania Academy of Fine Art, Philadelphia. Marin spent most of four years in Paris where Edward Steichen discovered his water colors and sent some of them to Alfred Stieglitz in New York, hailing them as "about as good as anything in that line that has ever been done." Stieglitz, like Steichen a photographer, ran the avantgarde New York art gallery "291," where he gave Marin a show in 1909. Marin was represented at the 1913 Armory Show with ten water colors of subjects taken from the skyscrapers of New York, Tyrol and the Adirondacks. Throughout most of his uneventful life, Marin spent his summers on the coast of Maine and his winters in his home in New Jersey overlooking the Manhattan skyline.

His favorite medium was water color. Even when he used oil, he employed it is a thin, transparent manner. He always sought to translate nature's light and movement into architectonic constructions of shimmering radiant colors, combining accuracy with spontaneity. Marin learned from Cézanne, Matisse and the Fauves, but also from Winslow Homer. He was in Paris at the time of the earliest Cubist experiments and his work contains Cubist elements as well as much that can be described as Expressionist. Yet, while his composition often veered towards abstraction, his lyrical color remained, on the whole, naturalistic.

Marin's favorite subjects were rocks, the sun and coast of Maine, and the skyscrapers and elevated trains of New York City. He recreated the poetry and drama he found in these motifs by simplifying objects into harmonies of pure, radiant colors. He once explained that his works were meant as "constructed expressions of the inner senses, responding to things seen and felt." He so perfected this technique that he sometimes dashed off a picture within minutes. "It is like golf," he said, "the fewer strokes I can take, the better the picture." Also, as if anticipating the Abstract Expressionists, he wrote, "Using paint *as* paint is different from using paint to paint a picture. I'm calling my pictures this year 'Movements in Paint' and not movements of boat, sea, or sky, because in these new paintings, although I use objects, I am representing paint first of all and not the motif primarily."

It took the public many years to discover the poetry in the direct calligraphy of his brushwork and the fluid nuance of his tones. Many who deplored his disintegrated forms and erratic lines ultimately learned to appreciate the impact created by the writhing shapes and passionate strokes and blots.

SEA PIECE

1951 · Oil on canvas · 22 x 28 inches · Whitney Museum of American Art, New York
(Gift of the Friends of the Whitney Museum of American Art)

Although the artist was over eighty when he painted this, it maintains the power and sureness of his earlier paintings. Like Raoul Dufy, he often treated the heavy pigments of oil in this swift, attenuated manner, and the influence of Cubism is still noticeable in the dissection of the composition into severely geometric patterns. Yet Marin is a highly individual painter.

JOHN MARIN · SEA PIECE

Oui, Oui, Oui

Composition on Yellow Ground

WOLS · 1913—1951

Wolfgang Schulze, who shortened his name to Wols, emigrated to Paris from Germany at the age of nineteen and died there in 1951. His brief artistic career was devoted to drawings and paintings in water color and oil—intuitive statements which served no preconceived intention. These paintings were not important to Wols for their own sake or as a means of success but as a kind of unquestioned activity that was part of this way of living. If his somewhat grotesque creations are accessible at all as pictures, either through their form or their color, it is because his spontaneous technique was unconsciously but surely guided by his innate artistry.

THE BLUE PHANTOM
1951 · Oil · 28³/₄ x 23⁵/₈ inches · Collection Madame Wols, Paris

Like a being from another world beyond human experience yet remarkably close to it, the dark violet "phantom" emerges from the infinite vastness of the blue space in which it exists. It is surrounded by a red and yellow aura and emits feelerlike rays from light holes. These rays are scratched in the paint with the brush handle in a manner characteristic of Wols.

184

WOLS · THE BLUE PHANTOM

Perspectives

The Burning Giraffe

SALVADOR DALI · 1904—

Dali was born in Figueras near Barcelona. Even as a student at the Madrid Academy (1921—24) he displayed the propensity for exaggerated personal behavior and for metaphysical and surrealist elements in his painting that are still characteristic of him. He enthusiastically learned the old masters' realistic, representational methods but has never used them for purely imitative purposes. At first his painting inclined toward the *Pittura Metafisica* of Chirico, later, in the late-1920's, toward Surrealism. Theatrics and notoriety accompanied him wherever he went. Out of scraps of brutally depicted reality and fragments of the irreality of dreams and hallucina-

tions he pieced together a sort of waxworks world. Its gruesomeness appals the viewer; it propels him from one sensation to another until he doubts the validity of logic and reason; it shocks him, yet attracts him with an extraordinary magical appeal stemming from the utterly realistic technique.

When Dali went to live in the United States he turned toward a mystically inclined "surreality" which expressed itself in religious subjects. He also began to paint portraits. He continues to produce excellent works in his native Spain, and holds a unique and controversial position in world art.

CHRIST OF ST. JOHN OF THE CROSS
1951 · Oil · 87³/₈ x 45 inches · Art Gallery and Museum, Glasgow

In a light-dark technique reminiscent of Baroque painting, Christ on the cross is depicted in a bold bird's-eye view, as though suspended against the darkness of the night sky. Does He hang as a constant reminder of Doomsday above the tiny strip of peaceful human world (made dubious nonetheless by its unreal colors) that

has, as it were, sidled into the picture? Or does His luminous form signify hope of redemption from the earthly vale of tears? We do not know. This ambivalence, containing threat and hope in equal measure, makes Him a true symbol of the revelation of St. John. This painting provides a good example of Dali's special magic.

SALVADOR DALI · CHRIST OF ST. JOHN OF THE CROSS

The Suburb

Joan of Arc

GEORGES ROUAULT · 1871—1958

Rouault, whose father was a Parisian cabinetmaker, was interested in painting even in childhood. His father and maternal grandfather passed on to him their liking for the paintings of Daumier, Courbet and Manet, and the boy's inclination for art met no resistance. When he was fourteen he was apprenticed to a maker of stained glass named Hirsch, and this proved to be a significant period in his life which largely determined the course of his own painting. In 1891 he gave up glass painting and for the next five years attended the École des Beaux-Arts. He won several prizes and awards for his paintings, most of which were on religious themes, but failed to win the coveted Prix de Rome. Embittered, he left the École des Beaux-Arts and, driven perhaps by a spiritual need arising out of his material poverty, turned to themes which provided an outlet for his pent-up bitterness: merciless exposures of man's corrupt face and his fall from grace. Under the influence of his friend Léon Bloy he began to paint prostitutes and circus people and all the wretchedness of the world in gloomy, nocturnal colors. Yet Rouault was a deeply religious man, and the dark side of human life was not important to him for its own sake or as a subject for social criticism but because its inhabitants too will partake of redemption. By traversing the depths of human existence he gained the freedom to indulge his lifelong love for religious subjects with greater intensity.

About 1905, under the influence of Matisse, Rouault's palette began to take on an almost Fauve richness. Odalisques, clowns and social themes temporarily replaced religious subjects, which did not reappear until about 1913. In 1917, at the urging of the art dealer Ambroise Vollard, Rouault gave up painting for almost ten years to devote himself to book illustration. Not until 1928 did he begin to paint prolifically again, and now his unfinished paintings were completed in his most characteristic manner. The colors are concentrated within a framework of thick black lines suggestive of the lead strips used in stained-glass windows. For all their density, these colors have a stained-glass quality, although Rouault applied the paint ever more thickly, until in the end he was using an impasto technique that often made the canvas look like a relief. Nevertheless right to the end, even in his last pictures which are monumental in size, he retained what has always been the essential element in his work: spiritualization in an almost Gothic manner.

INTIMITÉ CHRÉTIENNE, CHRIST ET ENFANTS
1952 · Oil · 28⅝ x 40½ inches · Private Collection

Rouault liked to express himself in religious themes; their apartness from the hectic bustle of everyday life and their solemnity suited his emotional temperament. His religious pictures, of which this plate is an example, bring out the striking closeness of his painting to medieval stained glass as well as the remarkable luminosity of his colors.

GEORGES ROUAULT · INTIMITÉ CHRÉTIENNE,
CHRIST ET ENFANTS

Color Perspective

The Stuffed Bird
Solomon R. Guggenheim Museum,
New York

JACQUES VILLON · 1875—1963

Jacques Villon, born in Damville, Normandy, came of an artistic family. One of his brothers, Raymond Duchamp-Villon, was a sculptor; another brother, Marcel Duchamp, and his sister Suzanne Duchamp were painters, and he himself had a strong talent for drawing. He was trained in the studio of Cormon in Paris and in the 1890's some of his drawings were published in Parisian jounals. His liking for graphic art was certainly one reason for his joining the Cubist movement in 1911; he put this shift in position on record, so to speak, by founding the *Section d'Or*, a group of artists whose members included Francis Picabia, Roger de la Fresnaye and Albert Gleizes. Determined to realize Cézanne's desire to make Impressionism into something durable like the art in the museums, Villon constructed his paintings out of geometrical forms and the pure hues of the color scale, thus giving them a kind of crystalline clarity. About 1919 he turned to abstraction, but he never relinquished his characteristic style and color or his geometrical construction.

SPRING
1952 · Oil on canvas · 28¹/₂ x 23¹/₈ inches · Private Collection

This abstract hymn to spring, which suggests a collage composed of tiny rectilinear color planes, is a masterpiece of color and construction. It is full of upward movement symbolizing growth; the spatters of color spurting from the pointed form on the lower edge of the picture suggest a fountain. The effect of blossoming and growth is achieved primarily by the organization of larger planes of more intense color in the lower half of the picture, balanced in the upper half by smaller color areas which have been made light and permeable by "empty" patches of white. The total effect is one of lightness and airiness.

JACQUES VILLON · SPRING

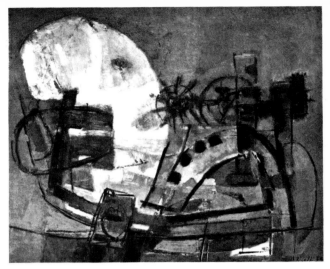

Adriatic

Lightning Strikes the Hill

RENATO BIROLLI · 1906—1959

Renato Birolli, born in Verona, belonged to the school of modern Italian painting associated with Giuseppe Santomaso, Bruno Cassinari and Antonio Corpora. These artists attempt to present a personal vision of nature. In Birolli's works nature and the subject matter (which Birolli usually identifies in the title) are of little importance in themselves. They merely provide pointers which the painter weaves into the complex of colors and forms he creates to express his own personal vision. Representational indications or symbols of them crop up here and there, helping the viewer to bridge the gap between the world of the picture and the natural world transformed into artistic vision. Nevertheless the artist's true subject is the canvas he presents to the viewer.

GREEN AND BLUE OVER LIGURIA
1952 · Oil · 35⁷/₈ x 24¹/₂ inches · Collection Achille Cavellini, Brescia

Green, blue, dull patchy red, and dark, shadowy violet contained within a framework of planes and lines, denote Liguria—or rather the essence of Liguria as it presented itself to the painter, stripped of all objective associations. The whole feel of the Ligurian coast is there: the green of the land, the blue of the water and the clear, cloudless sky. The painting contains shorthand signs for house, tower and boat. However far these may be from what the eye actually sees, they offer a starting point from which the sensuous totality of this landscape, distilled into the interplay of color and form, becomes accessible to the viewer.

192

RENATO BIROLLI · GREEN AND BLUE OVER LIGURIA

Dutch Town
Solomon R. Guggenheim Museum,
New York

Navigable Space

GUSTAVE SINGIER · 1909—

Gustave Singier, a native of Belgium, was taken to Paris when he was ten. He was trained as an interior decorator and worked in this field until 1936. His professional experience with color and shapes and his hobby of painting from nature both left their mark on his work. When his friend Walch persuaded him to devote himself entirely to art—and more specifically to abstract painting—his aim was to translate the visible reality of the world around him into an inwardly perceived reality, much as his friend Alfred Manessier was doing.

Singier paints landscapes—if we can call them that—which translate nature into a completely subjective, lyrical pictorial world composed of carefully chosen color harmonies, tending toward blue, and firm, clearly outlined forms. Although his works lack the warmth of Manessier's brilliant colors, they have a direct appeal and communicate the painter's vision to the viewer without help from the title.

SPRINGTIME IN PARIS
1952 · Oil on canvas · 51¹/₂ x 38¹/₆ inches · Private Collection

Spring and all it stands for—the sprouting grass and the self-renewal of nature—are tellingly captured in this composition. There is certainly a temptation to see natural objects in the play of ribbonlike forms made up of color planes of gray and violet with touches of yellow, black and orange, but it is quickly repressed as we respond to the challenge of the springlike color harmonies.

194

GUSTAVE SINGIER · SPRINGTIME IN PARIS

Self-Portrait
Solomon R. Guggenheim Museum,
New York

Self-Portrait
Solomon R. Guggenheim Museum,
New York

FRANZ KLINE · 1910—1962

Kline was one of the most original and talented personalities in American art after 1945. Like Robert Motherwell, but even more consistently, he renounced color and expressed himself completely in black and white, painting grillelike structures of what look like massive intersecting beams or girders, executed in broad black bars and utilizing the play of the white spaces between them. Kline's designs, which somehow always give an impression of order, are not the product of an organizing will, as Mondrian's patterns are. His forms were set down on the canvas impulsively, just as they took shape during the unpremeditated act of painting. They reflect the painter's dynamic reaction to the challenge of the emerging painting. Nor are the white spaces mere incidental by-products of no artistic value. On the contrary, they heighten the feeling of energy concentrated in the black beams; they seem to be blocking something off or interrupting something; they make corners look sharper, edges more angular, and are thus as important as the black forms.

PAINTING NUMBER SEVEN

1952 · Oil · 56¹/₂ x 80 inches · Solomon R. Guggenheim Museum, New York

Although this elementally forceful color image consists solely of a few angular black beams, it is extraordinarily dynamic. The black tracklike forms seem to break into the picture space from the right and to collide with the verticals, which float freely against the white background, meeting a resistance which telescopes them, snaps them off sharply, forces them apart and downward. Of course this is just one of many possible interpretations. However we read this pattern, we cannot escape the feeling that what it communicates is not rigid immobility but action concentrated in a few powerful shapes and their interaction with the white areas.

FRANZ KLINE · PAINTING NUMBER SEVEN

Landscape

Composition

NICOLAES DE STAËL · 1914—1955

Nicolaes de Staël was born in St. Petersburg (now Leningrad) and died in France, at Antibes, forty-one years later. He devoted his short career to reconciling his vigorous love of natural things and the world the eye sees with an urge toward non-objective painting freed from any commitment to the visible. While he did not succeed in this ultimately insoluble task, he did in the end find a compromise that enabled him to produce paintings which are authentic as non-representational compositions while retaining references to nature. To be sure, he took all the body out of physical objects, reducing them to a kind of unreal astral existence.

HONFLEUR
1952 · Oil · Private Collection

Three horizontal zones compose a picture which, if it were not for the title, might be taken for an abstract composition whose only *raison d'être* is the delicate balance of the color planes. The painter's stated intention to make this composition a symbol for a landscape changes everything dramatically. Now we immediately perceive the three zones in a representational sense: the lower band of violet merging into pink is the earth; the dark blue middle band, which is more briskly organized, is a sea; and the upper blue zone, which grows darker toward the top, is the sky. The heavy impasto reenforces the nonrepresentational qualities, however.

NICOLAES DE STAËL · HONFLEUR

Landscape with Rider   *The Depths*

JACKSON POLLOCK · 1912—1956

Jackson Pollock, who was born in Cody, Wyoming, and died in an automobile accident at the age of forty-four, was one of the most striking phenomena in contemporary American art. Some of his early studies and drawings, made between 1930 and 1934, were based on pictures of Rubens, El Greco and Tintoretto. In his mature art movement and energy are divorced from concrete objects and enter into the dynamics of drawing or painting, which is governed by the physical act itself. Pollock achieved this goal—obviously not his only one—in the mid-1940's after arriving at complete abstraction by way of the Expressionism of Mexican painting, avant-garde European movements and Surrealism. This led him to compositions in which he was no longer seeking but finding. At this point he did not allow the picture to take shape according to a preconceived plan but gave himself over to the act of painting, which stems from the unconscious, and permitted the picture to "happen" without conscious intervention.

"When I am in my painting, I'm not aware of what I'm doing. It is only after a sort of 'get acquainted' period that I see what I have been about," Pollock once said. To be *in the painting* meant for him being one with the act of painting, discarding the inhibiting barriers of reflection, throwing himself into the spontaneous event and giving pure expression to the emotion clamoring for release. He said that he wanted to express his feelings, not illustrate them. His technique was designed to allow him to become one with the picture. "My painting does not come from the easel ... On the floor I am more at ease. I feel nearer, more a part of the painting, since this way I can walk around it, work from the four sides and literally be *in* the painting." When he said this, Pollock had temporarily given up the traditional methods. Easel, palette and brushes were discarded; the canvas or board was placed on the floor and liquid paint was dripped into it straight from the can, with knives, spatulas or sticks, or applied in thick impasto. Alien materials—sand, slivers of glass, can lids, bottle tops—were incorporated into the pigment, which might include aluminum paint or enamel. In a kind of ecstatic dance he created paintings which look like chaotic landscapes of another world but which actually have a compositional completeness, being unified by the dynamics of the paint itself into self-contained entities.

NUMBER TWELVE
1952 · Oil, Duco and Devolac on canvas · 101 x 88 inches · Private Collection

This large-scale painting eludes explanatory description. It can only be felt as an emotional experience devoid of all narrative element which derives its powerful fascination solely from resonant colors and intensely dynamic forms.

JACKSON POLLOCK · NUMBER TWELVE

La Ville Minérale

Aix-en-Provence
Solomon R. Guggenheim Museum,
New York

MARIA ELENA VIEIRA DA SILVA · 1908—

Maria Elena Vieira da Silva was born in Lisbon. At the age of nineteen she went to Paris to study sculpture, but her training in Fernand Léger's studio soon convinced her that painting was her true vocation. Her marriage to the Hungarian painter Arpad Szenes was another factor in her decision to change fields.

She developed a personal style of great dynamism and clarity, especially after World War II, which she spent in South America.

Her abstract idiom is based on a framework of horizontal and vertical lines and clusters of lines which are given resonance by the patches of strong color filling their interstices like a mosaic. Vieira da Silva's work is slightly reminiscent of Klee in its musicality, though its tone is much more expressive. Her compositions achieve a splendid balance between static and dynamic forces, between picture-space and picture-plane.

COMPOSITION
1953 · Kunsthalle Hannover

This composition, freely suspended in a nebulous space, is constructed of clusters of lines, predominantly horizontal as the format requires, and small squares of bright color. It illustrates one of Vieira da Silva's essential characteristics: the ability to make her totally abstract painting evoke associations with real things. One imagines a backdrop of city buildings towering up on the edge of the sea and reflected in the water. All physical solidity gradually dissolves into the haziness of sea and air.

MARIA ELENA VIEIRA DA SILVA · COMPOSITION

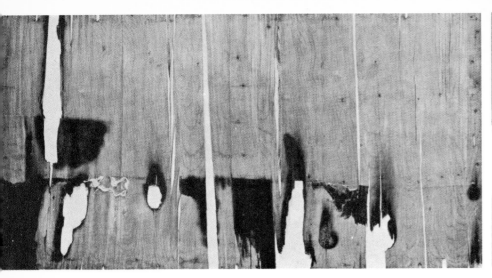

Wood and White I
Solomon R. Guggenheim Museum,
New York

Cloth and Black

ALBERTO BURRI · 1915—

Alberto Burri, an outstanding representative of contemporary Italian painting, was born in Città di Castello. After World War II he developed an Expressionist style into an extremely original abstract one. He organizes the canvas rigorously into large color planes something in the manner of Mondrian. Burri does not confine himself to conventional media and likes to introduce such things as scraps of burlap or other cloth, charred wood shavings and plastics. However much his pictures depend on color (which makes them paintings in the true sense), one of his primary motives is always to bring out the specific texture of alien materials and exploit their intrinsic charm to the full. He achieves handsome and sometimes unexpected results in this way.

CLOTH AND WHITE
1953 · Oil and glue on canvas and burlap · 38³/₈ x 22¹/₄ inches · Private Collection

The picture is composed of three irregularly outlined areas: a monochromatic black one, a white one, and a collage made of scraps of cloth in the lower right-hand third of the painting. The latter area is set off from the adjacent ones by its textures and also by the contrast of its lively patchwork and random splashes of paint. Our eyes cannot help being drawn to this mysteriously dynamic part of the painting—as the painter no doubt intended—and we are challenged to contrast its textures with the flatness of the painted areas. The composition is one of precise asymmetrical balance.

ALBERTO BURRI · CLOTH AND WHITE

Untitled

KYLE MORRIS · 1918—

After World War II the United States produced in Abstract Expressionism an independent art movement that has had a tremendous influence on the whole art world. Some important European painters, including Max Ernst, Fernand Léger, Joan Miró, and Piet Mondrian, who had been living in the United States during the war (chiefly in New York), played an important part in shaping and promoting this new movement. Its leaders were Jackson Pollock and Willem de Kooning, and by the 1950's their work was making itself felt in Europe and the rest of the world. Kyle Morris is one of the exponents of what came to be called action painting. He was born in Des Moines, Iowa, studied at the Art Institute of Chicago, taught at the Universities of Texas and California, but soon moved to New York to become a full-time painter. He has exhibited in many group and one-man shows.

BLUE AND BLACK
1953 · Oil on canvas · 53⁷/₈ x 79¹/₂ inches · Solomon R. Guggenheim Museum, New York

This masterly composition in cool tones of blue, black and gray clearly shows the influence of action painting on Morris' work. The picture crystallizes a moment in the artist's creative struggle; the viewer must see it as an actual event.

KYLE MORRIS · BLUE AND BLACK

Paulo Drawing   *The Torero's Table*

PABLO PICASSO · 1881—

Picasso was born in Malaga, Spain, where his father was a teacher of drawing. A a child he showed an extraordinary artistic talent, which his father encouraged, and at the age of fourteen he had already achieved such technical skill in drawing and painting that he successfully completed the works required for admission to the Barcelona school of art in one day instead of the allotted month. By the time he arrived in Paris in 1900 he had a sound technical background and had already chosen the subjects he was to concentrate on in his first great period, from 1901 to 1907: daily life and relations between the sexes. Living in poverty and moving back and forth between Paris and Barcelona, he painted first in the manner of late Impressionism with a profusion of shrill colors and then, about 1901, changed to the almost monochromatic palette of his blue period. Blue became a symbol of poverty, his own and that of the people he spoke for, people from the lowest levels of society. By the end of 1904 Picasso had established himself in Paris, and this tragic blue began to yield to the warm hues of his pink period. The spirit of his juggler and acrobat paintings is one of sensitive humanity rather than social *angst*.

Picasso's discovery of African sculpture about 1906 encouraged his tendency to stylization. He began to construct his pictures of monochromatic planes in a style parallel to Braque's but quite independent of it. This ultimately led him, with the famous "Demoiselles d'Avignon," painted in 1907, to Cubism. He then proceeded to exploit all conceivable potentialities and variations of this style until the early 1920's.

Next came another of the radical shifts so characteristic of Picasso—which are the real proof of his genius. While continuing to create Cubist pictures, he began also to paint lifelike human figures in the classical manner of Greek sculpture, as if trying to prove that he could handle a neoclassic style too. Soon came another change, as he introduced and merged Surrealist, Cubist, and symbolic elements in a full orchestration of his apparently inexhaustible inventiveness. He made a reputation in sculpture and, at Vallauris after World War II, in ceramics too. One thing, however, Picasso has never done: he has never pursued abstraction to the limit. Even in his Cubist paintings he never completely relinquished contact with visible reality.

SYLVETTE VIII
1954 · Oil · 45¹/₄ x 34³/₄ inches · Collection Pablo Picasso

In Vallauris in the summer of 1954 Picasso painted a series of more than a dozen profile portraits of a nineteen-year-old model named Sylvette David. The treatment ranges from representational to more or less abstract, and this painting falls midway between the two. All the girl's typical characteristics are shown: ponytail, austere but pretty features, long neck, but the subject as a whole is reduced to two-dimensional planes and planklike forms that immediately suggest Cubism.

PABLO PICASSO · SYLVETTE VIII

Chicago

Morning in the Forest

JEAN BAZAINE · 1904—

Bazaine, a native Parisian, is an art critic and theoretician as well as a painter. He started as a sculptor and when he began to paint it was in a representational style. Soon, however, he turned to abstraction, always seeking out the essential core (color) and significant form (shape and line) of his subject, dissociating these elements from nature, making them autonomous, and combining them in compositions of great force and energy. While his pictures seem to be completely abstract, actually they are always rooted in the visible—symbols of his reactions to the outward world. His works are rewarding no matter the level on which they are read.

SPAIN
1954 · Oil on canvas · Private Collection

The above notes on Bazaine's work are magnificently documented in this painting. What at first glance seems to be a patchwork of attractive colors suddenly takes shape when we read the title, though it is the fluid movement rather than the form that suggests Spain. To recognize how totally Spanish this composition of blue, red, ocher and white planes is, it is only necessary to try to associate it with Germany or France. But in the end it is the personal vision that is significant.

JEAN BAZAINE · SPAIN

For the Feast of Christ the King

February in Holland

ALFRED MANESSIER · 1911—

Manessier began as a representational painter, learning from the old masters as he copied their works in the Louvre. Under the influence of Roger Bissières (who also influenced many of Manessier's contemporaries) he turned to abstraction. Since he is a convinced Christian, it is not surprising that he should treat religious and sacred subjects: the Passion, the liturgy of the Mass or manifestations of the divine in the spiritual night which plunges man into darkness. But instead of presenting descriptive scenes or indulging in religious symbolism, Manessier translates religious experience into the language of form and color, freeing it from all associations with the material world. This explains why his work has a mystical, emotional impact rare in abstract painting.

NORTHERN SPRINGTIME
1954 · Oil · 50³/₄ x 63¹/₈ inches · Private Collection

This composition of carefully outlined forms and colors designed to harmonize with the dominant bluish green realizes its full effect in the horizontal format so favored by Manessier. The shapes are richly traced with a latticework of drawing and sometimes divided up into small blocks of different colors accented in red and green. They seem to flow or hover, no doubt intended to offer a striking contrast to the motionless tranquillity of the green background. The leftward thrust of the central birdlike form is answered and contained by the shapes along the upper and lower edges, so that the whole picture conveys an impression of concentrated movement which reaches its height at the edges of the canvas and finds a counterpart in the resonance of the colors.

ALFRED MANESSIER · NORTHERN SPRINGTIME

Composition
Solomon R. Guggenheim Museum,
New York

Composition (Red-Blue-Orange)

SERGE POLIAKOFF · 1906—1969

Poliakoff was born in Moscow, but later lived in Paris. Over the years his paintings evoled into compositions of large, simply defined color planes. Straight or jagged outlines dominate the rarer rounded ones, making the mood of the pictures aggressive rather than gentle or melodious. But the aggressiveness never gets out of hand; it is restrained by Poliakoff's color, which for all its boldness is used in subtle tonalities that have a tranquillizing effect. His compositions reveal a combination of strength and sensitivity.

COMPOSITION IN BLUE-GREEN
1954—1955 · Oil · 28¹/₂ x 23³/₈ inches · Private Collection

The darkest and lightest colors in this picture are anchored in the central cluster of irregular shapes. The panels of color in delicately harmonized shades of blue and green that fill the rest of the canvas focus upon this group. Their dark values make it stand out with crystalline brilliance, while their notably cool mood prevents it from becoming too self-assertive or strident.

SERGE POLIAKOFF · COMPOSITION IN BLUE-GREEN

Night Square

Detour

WILLEM DE KOONING · 1904—

Willem de Kooning is one of the most important and influential figures in contemporary American painting. Born in Rotterdam in 1904, he was apprenticed to a firm of painters and decorators and received his artistic training at the academies of Rotterdam and Brussels and the Antwerp school of design. He emigrated to the United States in 1926 and in the early 1940's was among the leading avant-garde painters. Since his first retrospective show in 1948 his name has ranked with that of Jackson Pollock as an original painter of great expressivity.

A dedicated abstractionist, driven by a Van Gogh-like passion and a determination to transform and reshape material reality, de Kooning is nonetheless also guided by a co-ordinating clarity and constructive vision something like Piet Mondrian's. One might simply say that he is engaged in a never-ending struggle to let form survive in a space that is constantly subject to fluid movement—a valid symbol for the situation of modern man and his insecurity in a crumbling world. It is not difficult to see why in 1949 human figures reappeared for a few years in de Kooning's deliberately unstructured pictorial world of rectangular and conical forms and tangles of crooked lines. But the theme of "woman," to which he then turned, was not a means of escaping from abstraction. On the contrary, he was trying to master objective reality through abstraction. His aim was not to describe what the eye sees but to depict the motif as influenced by chance and instinctive reactions.

Although de Kooning's "Woman" cycle ranks among his best work, his painting became more abstract again about 1953, when he seems to have found the constraint of objectivity too confining for his excited style.

COMPOSITION
1955 · Oil · 78³/₈ x 68¹/₄ inches · Solomon R. Guggenheim Museum, New York

Chaotic, full of the restless movement typical of de Kooning, flung on the canvas in an act of "engaged" painting totally involved in the creative event, this grandiose composition offers a good lead for discovering what de Kooning is trying to do. In the confusing interplay of brushstrokes and lines one feels the color planes striving toward independence, though they never manage to achieve complete freedom and firm shape. Stability and dynamic change balance one another.

WILLEM DE KOONING · COMPOSITION

Promenade　　　　　　　　　　　*The Staircase*

MASSIMO CAMPIGLI · 1895—

Along with such artists as Gino Severini, Massimo Campigli, a Florentine by birth but a Parisian by adoption, belongs to the "generation of masters" who made Italy's truly significant contribution to the art of the first half of the twentieth century. Campigli's work represents an attempt to master and define visible reality.

The diversity of nature is transformed into simple physical images organized in a rigorous yet decorative structure. His painting is also marked by a massiveness and archaic simplicity of form not unlike Giorgio de Chirico's, though he restrains this tendency for the sake of a more pleasing effect.

TOWN IN THE MIDI
1956 · Oil · 28¹/₂ x 21 inches · Private Collection

The construction of this tightly organized painting is determined by the geometry of the background. The verticals dominate the horizontals, and the central axis stands out as the main focus. Along this axis Campigli has placed a statuesque rather than lifelike figure of a woman. Her elongated body is distorted to show frontal and side views, her head is in full profile. The narrative element is subordinated to Campigli's desire to make everything part of a strong rhythm, to present things quietly and essentially and bring out their inherent value. This desire also dominates the color, whose dull, earthy or stonelike tones are appropriate to a kind of painting that seeks essential form. The artist has achieved absolutely quiet monumentality.

218

MASSIMO CAMPIGLI · TOWN IN THE MIDI

Study for a Rider   *Acrobat Family*

MARINO MARINI · 1901—

Marino Marini was born in Pistoia, studied painting and sculpture at the Florence Academy and began his artistic career with painting and graphics. In 1928, however, he switched to sculpture, which proved to be his true field and where he made his reputation.

In both media he remained equally committed to nature, though he reshaped it artistically and reduced it to essentials. Both his paintings and his statues demonstrate the same pronounced sense of materiality.

HORSE WITH ACROBATS
1956 · Oil · 58¹/₂ x 46⁷/₈ inches · Private Collection

The human figures and the horse, seen in front view, are reduced to their simplest forms, like a group of statues recalling the angularity of Marini's own sculpture. We are almost unaware of the action going on at the right, where one of the acrobats is hoisting another to his shoulder. The fanciful color of each of the flat, two-dimensional bodies has been selected with an eye to the total color complex. Although these colors are not modeled in any way and have no dimension of depth, they somehow make the bodies look heavy and solid. A work of sculpture has been translated into paint.

MARINO MARINI · HORSE WITH ACROBATS

Still Life

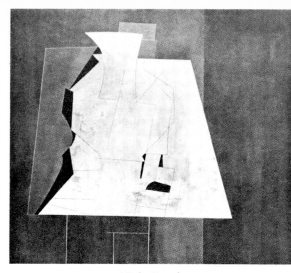

Night Facade
Solomon R. Guggenheim Museum,
New York

BEN NICHOLSON · 1894—

Ben Nicholson, the son of William Nicholson, a well-known English Impressionist painter, was born near Uxbridge. Although his early work was more or less traditional, since 1945 he has been England's leading abstract painter. His style, rooted in a strong dislike for theory and dogmatism of any kind, is almost unequalled in range; his subjects include complete abstractions in the manner of Piet Mondrian as well as natural objects and happenings. Yet while visible reality has its place in his pictures, it is never there for the sake of its descriptive value, but as a world which to him is neither more nor less "objective" than the abstractions of non-objective painting. Nicholson does not recognize any distinction between reality and abstraction. To him both are equally valuable, since both can be used as vehicles of communication and stripped of all functions except their artistic one within the given painting. He has said himself that the kind of painting he finds exciting is not necessarily either objective or non-objective. It is, however, both musical and architectonic, and the architectural structure serves to express a "musical" relationship between form, tone and color.

COMPOSITION
1957 · Oil · 65¹/₈ x 47⁵/₈ inches · Private Collection

This picture, composed of the interplay of two-dimensional planes interwoven with a few lines, shows how strongly Nicholson has been influenced by Mondrian. It also shows how serious he was when he called art "a self-sufficient force" which, without recourse to the seen world, organizes "objective" forms or color planes to create its own individual values: spatial, colorful and rhythmic harmonies. Applying this to "Composition," we see that through form and color he has created a self-contained pictorial world.

BEN NICHOLSON · COMPOSITION

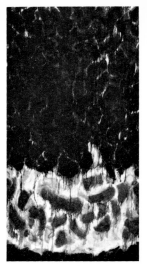

Red and Black
Solomon R. Guggenheim Museum,
New York

The Over Yellow

SAM FRANCIS · 1923—

Sam Francis was born in San Mateo, California, in 1923 and moved to Paris since 1950. He started out as a student of psychology and medicine and began to study art under Clifford Still in the late 1940's. Francis is an action painter like Jackson Pollock, but his paintings are more deliberately organized and composed. They are usually large in format. About 1954 his monochromatic tonalities gave way to bright, serene colors carefully co-ordinated with large patches of white, unpainted canvas to create a magically brilliant world of amoebalike splashes, dribbles, flecks, and blurred dabs of paint. This color seems to be scattered over the "atmospheric" space of the background like a light fall of snow, although the drippings of the thin paint give the whole composition a striking effect of reaching upward beyond the upper edge of the canvas into the space outside the picture.

SUMMER NUMBER ONE
1957 · Oil · Martha Jackson Gallery, New York

Patches of transparent color and dribbles of paint suggesting the air roots of tropical plants are suspended like a bunch of unreal flowers in the infinite vastness of the picture-space. Far from being meaningless or devoid of action, the unpainted background is an indispensable part of the picture, as in Chinese ink paintings. It provides an existential space for the play of colors without which this mysteriously shimmering color-cloud would never have been able to take form.

SAM FRANCIS · SUMMER NUMBER ONE

Site aux Errances

*Door with Couch Grass
Solomon R. Guggenheim Museum,
New York*

JEAN DUBUFFET · 1901—

Jean Dubuffet was born in Le Havre in 1901. It was only in 1942 that he decided, after considerable uncertainty, to make painting his career. His style is a reaction against all formal tradition and conventional taste, and his work sometimes becomes a proving ground for new techniques and media. Dubuffet derived great stimulus from his early interest in the art of children, mentally disturbed people and untrained amateurs. In 1947 he exhibited in his own gallery, the Foyer de l'Art Brut, a collection of such works, assembled from most European countries over a period of twenty years. For him this *art brut* (or unpolished art) is superior to most conventional art and certainly more honest. It has had a formative influence on his own work, which for many years was a somewhat grotesque sign language with a lurking humor.

During the 1950's and early 1960's Dubuffet's total rejection of tradition led him to invent a number of daring techniques. He would cut up painted canvas and arrange the scraps in a sort of mosaic, piece together dried leaves and flowers in similar compositions, and use papier-mâché and aluminum foil as media for works which thus became strangely alienated from the conventional craftsmanship of painting.

LANDSCAPE
1957 · Gouache, paper, butterfly wings · 13⁷/₈ x 8¹/₂ inches · Private Collection

Dubuffet's determination to incorporate all kinds of alien materials into his paintings has made "Landscape" a unique picture. Patches of gouache color in yellow, ocher, brown and black, applied in the technique of action painting, are overlaid with a scattering of glued-on butterfly wings. Ignoring the question whether this may not be a lapse of taste and too much of a good thing, we are forced to admit that the total color effect has its charm. Dubuffet's compositions reveal much more than a surface attraction, however.

JEAN DUBUFFET · LANDSCAPE

Painting

Painting
Solomon R. Guggenheim Museum,
New York

PIERRE SOULAGES · 1919—

Soulages was born in Rodez and later went to live in Paris. He has developed an abstract style with a stong preference for solid, structured form. His paintings are composed of heavy, stable-looking shapes, usually in black, which suggest building blocks or calligraphic symbols, freely suspended in the picture-space. But these units are not built up into solid architectural structures; they are, as it were, lapped in atmosphere and thus seem to exist in a remarkably elastic environment.

COMPOSITION
1958 · Oil · 35¹/₂ x 25³/₈ inches · Private Collection

Horizontal bars, stacked on top of and behind each other, stretch across the painting. An ocher-brown light breaks in from below, catching the lower edges of these massive, planklike bodies. The gray forms projecting from the chinks between the deep black planes also seem to catch the light, and at the top of the picture a white gleam suggests a concealed window. All this gives the composition the depth and richness of atmosphere characteristic of Soulages.

PIERRE SOULAGES · COMPOSITION

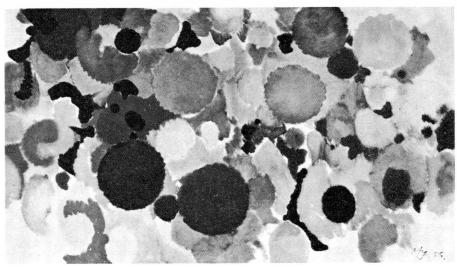

Composition with Butterflies   *Chromaticism Strong and Tender*

ERNST WILHELM NAY · 1902—1968

Ernst Wilhelm Nay, a Berliner who later lived in Cologne, was one of the most distinctive personalities in contemporary German art. At first he painted realistically in the manner of Karl Hofer, but in the 1930's under the influence of Ernst Ludwig Kirchner he began to show a delight in decorative elements and in the expressiveness of non-representational color, which were to become the signature of his increasingly abstract style. About 1950 the semi-representa-tional forms in his paintings began to be replaced by precisely designed complexes of imaginative form: beadlike strings, pointed ovals, fanlike shapes, in which color, whether in areas or small touches, came increasingly to dominate the graphic element. In 1955 Nay's "disc" period began. Carefully co-ordinated circles of color were then integrated into harmonious compositions of a beauty unmatched elsewhere in his work.

MELAGRANA
1958 · Oil · 63¼ x 50⅝ inches · Private Collection

Any thematic analysis of this composition of amorphous patches of color would be meaningless. The mind schooled in representational art will find nothing to catch hold of here. All we are aware of is an experience stemming from the mysterious interaction and rhythmic contrasts of patches of color clustering together like amoebas. Yet what looks so chaotic has its own order, as we immediately realize if we try in our imagination to eliminate or shift a single patch of color, reverse the tensions created by the juxtaposition of red and green, black and orange, or change the position of the ocher disc to which the eye is magically drawn.

230

ERNST WILHELM NAY · MELAGRANA

The Fiddler   *The Clock*

MARC CHAGALL · 1887—

Chagall was born in 1887 to Jewish parents in Vitebsk, Russia. He began to study painting in 1907 at the Imperial Academy of St. Petersburg and in 1910 went to Paris, where he found living quarters in La Ruche, an artists' apartment house where Amedeo Modigliani and Fernand Léger also lived. He soon made a wide circle of friends including artists, poets (among them Apollinaire) and writers and began a joyous encounter with the latest trends in French painting, especially Cubism. His style, however, was only marginally affected by Cubism's rationality; it had some effect on his themes, and his form became firmer under its influence. The essential characteristic of Chagall's painting was an utterly poetic, dreamy vision, a blend of childhood memories, ghetto life and Hassidism, the kind of Jewish pantheism that sees man in constant community with God. Heedless of his friends' skepticism and inebriated with color, he created a fairytale world surpassing in fantasy anything known to the West. In this world all relationships were reversible, remembered time merged with the present and the future, solid bodies became transparent, and man and animals entered into memorable symbioses. Artistically it represented an unparalleled synthesis of Cubism, Expressionism and Surrealism.

In 1914 Chagall went back to Russia, and World War I prevented him from returning to France until 1922. In the meantime he became Commissar of Visual Arts for the District of Vitebsk and founded a government academy in his native city. Back in Paris, he began to produce graphics comparable to his paintings in significance. Between 1923 and 1927 he made ninety-six etchings to illustrate Gogol's *Dead Souls,* between 1927 and 1930 a hundred and two illustrating La Fontaine's *Fables.* These were commissioned by his long-time patron Ambroise Vollard, who in 1931 asked him to do a series of graphic illustrations for the Bible, for which a visit to Palestine, Syria and Egypt provided stimulus.

Chagall was deeply disturbed by the Jewish pogroms in Germany and the threat of war. His style aquired a dramatic note, and in 1941 he took advantage of an invitation from the New York Museum of Modern Art to escape from ever-present danger. He lived a retired life in America until 1947, designing scenery and costumes for the ballet. In 1947 he returned to Paris, then went to live in Vence, where he took up ceramics. After that he produced a continuing stream of significant works, including stained-glass windows, a ceiling decoration for the Paris Opéra, and paintings for the New York Metropolitan Opera.

THE BOUQUET
1959 · Gouache and Pastel · 16⁵/₈ x 12⁷/₈ inches · Private Collection

The picture centers on a huge bouquet of nondescript flowers which seems about to break out of the confines of the canvas. From a blue-green center clusters of flowers shoot outward like the spurting stars of rockets. A little bird adds an idyllic touch. Reality is transposed into a dream world by a goat's head in an unreal bluish green and a big hand which cannot be brought into any normal relationship with the white profile of the girl whose hair has turned into a curious Christlike figure.

MARC CHAGALL · THE BOUQUET

T-50 Painting 8
Solomon R. Guggenheim Museum,
New York

Painting

HANS HARTUNG · 1904—

Hans Hartung, a native of Leipzig, first visited Paris in 1925; after World War II he became a French citizen and a Parisian. He turned to non-objective painting in the early 1920's and has been an abstract painter ever since. His style is often close to action painting (in his drawings for instance) but not identical with it. His colors are usually restrained, often confined to black, white and gray; his pictures are composed of overlapping background areas differentiated by colors and linear patterns. Hartung's work often shows a tinge of romanticism and expressive gesture which mysteriously communicate themselves to the viewer.

T 1962—U 4
1962 · Oil · 70 x 43¹/₄ inches · Private Collection

Although this picture is limited in color to blue and brown, it derives extraordinary life from the sophisticated gradations from dark to light in the brown area, which seems to be suspended above a blue background. This effect is heightened by the dry brush technique, which makes the bright vertical strokes look like hanging hair and gives the brown area the appearance of a mass consisting of transparent layers and remarkably suggestive of space. The final effect is a mysterious one.

234

HANS HARTUNG · T 1962—U 4

Au Lapin Agile

Saint Tropez

BERNARD BUFFET · 1928—

Bernard Buffet, a Parisian, is considered the outstanding representative of a group of young French artists who came to the fore after World War II with paintings in a representational style. Buffet was dissatisfied with the instruction at the École des Beaux-Arts and at the age of eighteen began to go his own way—from which he has never turned back. He once said that every age needs artists to portray it and record it for the future. Portraying it meant, for him and his like-minded colleagues, turning back to nature. Buffet creates documentary pictures without falling into mere imitation or trying to reproduce the minute details of things he paints. Atmospherically transfigured space has no place in his paintings, which seem peculiarly airless; his colors are watery and transparent. Non-essentials are eliminated; his statement deals with the universal and the enduring. Draftsmanship plays such an important part in his work that his paintings often look like tastefully tinted prints or drawings.

GRAND CANAL
1962 · Oil · Private Collection

Without being atmospheric in the naturalistic sense, this view of the famous Cà d'oro on the Grand Canal in Venice has the tang of damp sea air. The Palazzo, a gem of Venetian Gothic, is realistically drawn with the brush, while the busy details of the arcades, windows, moldings, gables, and pinnacles are reduced to their essentials.

BERNARD BUFFET · GRAND CANAL

The Red Stairs

The Funeral
Whitney Museum of American Art,
New York

BEN SHAHN · 1898—1969

Ben Shahn was born in Lithuania, came to the United States at the age of eight, served an apprenticeship in lithography, and then worked as a commercial artist. His commercial experience had a strong and permanent influence on his work, giving him a lasting appreciation of craftsmanship and making drawing an essential element in his painting. He began to study painting in 1922 at the National Academy of Design and in two visits to France was inspired by Georges Rouault. In the early 1930's he began to acquire his own style.

Shahn's central theme was man in his social deprivation, manipulated by political arbitrariness. His ideas always had a sound psychological basis, and he expressed them forcefully, although his paintings rarely have the stridency of German Expressionism. Their emotional impact is tempered by their simplicity of form and by the restraining graphic elements, which produce subdued but powerful quietness. Shahn could express himself as effectively on a small scale as in huge murals. His graphic work strongly influenced American poster design, especially during the 1940's.

LUTE WITH MOLECULES
1964 · Gouache · 27 x 40¹/₂ inches · Collection Mr. and Mrs. Lew Fergenson

This "still life" of a lute or mandolin brings out the poster-designer and graphic artist in Shahn. Two color areas, one reddish-brown, the other light blue, are superimposed on the white background.

They are enlivened with lines, dots and circles which resolve themselves into forms (the musical instrument) or abstract patterns. They invite scrutiny rather than interpretation.

BEN SHAHN · LUTE WITH MOLECULES

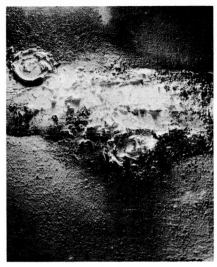

Polarity   *The Take-off I*

THÉO KERG · 1909—

Théo Kerg, a native of Luxembourg, likes to say that he was born on October 4, 1929, meaning that his life as an artist began on that date, when he went to live in Paris at the age of twenty. He studied architecture, painting and sculpture at the École des Beaux-Arts and art history and philosophy at the Sorbonne, earning a precarious living as a tutor and by copying paintings in the Louvre. At the end of 1932 he went to Dusseldorf to study with Paul Klee. This brief visit ended in March, 1933, when violent attacks by the Nazis forced him to return to Paris, but it was perhaps his most formative experience. It gave him the confidence to enter a field which already attracted him: abstraction.

Considering the range of his training, one is not surprised that Kerg should have worked consistently toward a type of painting that goes beyond the interaction of colors, adding tactile experiences to visual ones. Tactilism, which he felt to be the style most suited to him, has remained peculiarly his own—in fact it was he who gave it its name; other painters have approached it only marginally. The aim of the style is to make tactile experience a sort of fourth dimension of painting, not through illusion but through tangible modeling of the canvas in plastic relief. Raised areas are formed on the canvas by adding sand, synthetic resin or similar substances to the paint and working it with a knife. Their undulations and curves, their fragmented or compact surfaces—in short their variegated relief—arouse impressions which combine with the effect of the frescolike color (usually held to a single hue) to convey what the artist is trying to communicate: the feeling of an explosion, say, or perhaps of insecurity. Being so close to sculpture, Tactile paintings need light to bring them to life even more than conventional ones do. In view of its mural quality it is not surprising that Kerg has utilized Tactilism in architecture.

HOMAGE TO COUPERIN
1964 · Oil · 28¹/₂ x 23³/₈ inches · Private Collection

In the 1960's Kerg took to engraving words or texts into his pictures. The shapes of the letters enliven the surface, and the words serve as a kind of explanation of the painting, to which they are directly linked by meaning.